I DREAMED I WAS A VERY CLEAN TRAMP

ALSO BY RICHARD HELL

THE VOIDOID
ARTIFACT
GO NOW
HOT AND COLD
GODLIKE

I DREAMED I WAS A VERY CLEAN TRAMP

AN AUTOBIOGRAPHY

RICHARD HELL

An Imprint of HarperCollinsPublishers

Pages 291–293 serve as a continuation of the copyright page.

The names of seven briefly appearing characters have been changed.

HarperCollins books may be purchased for educational, business, or sales promotional use. For information please write: Special Markets Department, Harper-Collins Publishers, 10 East 53rd Street, New York, NY 10022.

FIRST EDITION

Designed by Leah Carlson-Stanisic

Library of Congress Cataloging-in-Publication Data has been applied for.

ISBN 978-0-06-219083-3

13 14 15 16 17 OV/RRD 10 9 8 7 6 5 4 3 2 1

To Sheelagh and Ruby

I DREAMED I WAS A VERY CLEAN TRAMP

L ike many in my time, when I was little I was a cowboy. I had
chaps and a white straw cowboy hat and I tied my holsters to my
thighs with rawhide. I'd step out onto the porch and all could
see a cowboy had arrived.

This was in Lexington, Kentucky, when everybody was a kid. I
looked for caves and birds and I ran away from home. My favorite
thing to do was run away. The words "let's run away" still sound magic
to me.

My parents arrived in Lexington in 1948. They'd met two years before at Columbia University in New York, where they were graduate
students in psychology, and had married a year after that. When my
father, Ernest Meyers, who'd grown up in Pittsburgh, Pennsylvania,
got his Columbia PhD, he found a job teaching at the University of
Kentucky. I was born in late 1949. My ma postponed a career to take
care of the home.

Our family was just the four of us, including my sister, Babette, who
was born a year and a half after me. We felt close to my father's mother,
Grandma Linda, who lived in New York, and we occasionally visited
one of his brothers, Richard—a chemist for Texaco—and his wife and
kids, at their home near Poughkeepsie, but beyond that there wasn't

much awareness of family, or family history. I had no real understanding of what a Jew was, for instance, though I knew that my father's family fit that description somehow. I thought Judaism was a religion, and we didn't have any religion.

My mother, born Carolyn Hodgson, was an only child. Her mother, Dolly Carroll (born Dolly Griffin), whom we knew as Mama Doll, was a working-class Methodist lady from Alabama. She played bridge and liked a cocktail. She'd been married four times. We saw her for a few days once every three or four years. She and my mom's father, Lester

Ernest Meyers, 1948.

Hodgson, who'd owned a filling station in Birmingham until it went bust in the Depression, had divorced when my mother was a young child, and I only remember being in the same room with him two or three times.

We lived in the suburbs in America in the fifties. My roots are shallow. I'm a little jealous of people with strong ethnic and cultural roots. Lucky Martin Scorsese or Art Spiegelman or Dave Chappelle. I came from Hopalong Cassidy and Bugs Bunny and first grade at ordinary Maxwell Elementary.

I came from Hopalong Cassidy

In 1956, when I was six and we lived on Rose Street by the university, my father bought a cream and green 1953 Kaiser, which he drove to work every morning a mile down a street that ran between the big UK basketball arena and its football stadium. His campus workrooms were in an old tree-shaded red-brick building on the side of a hill. The classrooms, lab, and office there smelled of wood, chalk, wax, graphite, dust, fresh air, and armpits. The rooms were softly shadowed wood. Tree limbs swayed outside the windows. My father was an experimental psychologist; he didn't treat patients but observed animal behavior in labs. Small hard-rubber rat mazes lay on the tabletops among big manual typewriters. There were wooden glass-front cabinets against the walls, and rows of chair-desks facing the blackboards. That type of plain old academic building, or the one that housed the local school for the blind, where he did research on Braille, still feels like home to me, like a humble paradise, as little as I could ever stand schooling.

In the center of town stood a classic rough-hewn Romanesque courthouse, with an equestrian statue of Confederate general John Hunt Morgan out front. A few blocks further along Main Street lay the train station waiting shed, and in that same stretch Main's two cozy, plush movie houses, the Kentucky and the Strand, which were staffed with pimpled ushers and showed first-run double features and cartoons, including Saturday-morning all-cartoon programs. By the bus stop there was a Woolworth's dime store and a bakery that sold glazed doughnuts warm from the oven.

The limestone, pillared public library was in the middle of a heavily wooded park a few blocks behind the courthouse, across the street from Transylvania College ("the first college west of the Allegheny Mountains"). Inside, the library was marble, with sunshine from the second-story skylight brightening the ground floor's central information desk; whispers, shuffling shoe steps, and shelves and shelves of musty-smelling, dimpled green or orange library-bound books free for the taking.

On the outskirts of town were drive-in movies and an amusement park. The family would take grocery bags full of homemade popcorn to the drive-in, and, on the way home, my sister and I fit lengthwise, head to feet, in the backseat, asleep. Every once in a while we'd get to visit Joyland, where there was a wooden roller coaster and a merry-go-round and a funhouse and a Tilt-a-Whirl in the midst of game booths and cotton candy and hot dog stands among huge shade trees with picnic tables below them and starlings under those.

In the suburbs the houses were unlocked. There was no "air-conditioning" but fans. A big warehouse in a weathered industrial neighborhood towards town stocked fresh-cut blocks of ice yanked at a loading dock by giant tongs into newspapered car trunks to power iceboxes—though most people did own an electric refrigerator by then—or to fill coolers for picnics. You'd stab the slick crystal with picks till it cracked.

Once, as a teenager in Lexington, on a hot, clear summer day, I was in a stone hut in an open field with some friends. More friends clustered in the landscape outside like some Fragonard or Watteau painting—Fragonard crossed with Larry Clark—playing and talking. A guy's attention got caught by the sky. He stood in the high grass staring up, pointing and calling. We all craned our necks. There were specks in the sky floating down; chairs made of snow and snow couches touched down all around us. We were laughing and crying.

That happened in a dream a few years after I'd arrived in still-lonesome New York. I woke up ecstatic and grateful, my throat constricted and eyes overflowing.

In the winter of 1956, when I was in first grade, the family moved from the cottage on Rose Street to a new suburb, Gardenside, on the edge of town.

Nearly every lot in the tract was the same small size and there were only a few house designs, mostly two-bedroom. Each house had saplings in the same two spots on either side of the walk leading up to the front door and the same type of evergreen shrubbery under the living room picture windows facing the street. Our house was just like the classic child's drawing of a home, a red-brick box under a steep shingled roof that had a chimney on one end of it.

At the bottom of the street ran a creek. Lawns descended to border both sides of it, but along its banks uncut foliage grew thick and high. The most interesting thing about it was that it wasn't man-made. The idea that you could follow its path rather than the patterns imposed by people on everything else in sight was exciting. I remember first realizing that the creek might start and end anywhere, far off, that it didn't just exist in the area I knew. The thought was a glowing little diorama hidden inside my brain, kind of like Duchamp's *Étant donnés* (*Given: 1. The Waterfall, 2. The Illuminating Gas*).

Gardenside had farmland at its borders—tobacco and corn and livestock—and woods.

Our house was one of the first in the suburb to be completed, and the ongoing construction all around us for blocks was our playground.

One late afternoon that first year, there were only two of us left still messing around outside. We were trying to topple a big iron barrel that was filled to the brim with water. Finally we figured out a way of using wood scraps as levers and pushed it over.

Gardenside, on the edge of town

The street was empty. Roy Baker and I went and sat down in the rubble by the partly built house to talk things over. The building was just fresh four-by-tens across a cinder-block foundation with a few two-by-fours poking up where walls would go. The street was barren but littered with heaps and bristling, and smelled of fresh sawn wood, wet concrete, dirt, and burnt tar paper.

The men who were working here had seen us goofing around before they'd left for the day. By the time they'd gone, we were the only kids left. Tomorrow morning, they would realize it had been us who'd knocked over the barrel. Kids our age shouldn't be strong enough to turn over something as heavy as that. I explained this to Roy Baker, who was a few months younger than me. "They're going to think we're superhumanly strong. They'll want to put us in the circus. Think of how that will be, when we come out into the ring under the big top, the crowd waiting, and then we can't lift up the barbells! There is only one thing to do. We have to run away."

We walked and walked, further than we'd ever been, and stole some pennies from the dashboard of a parked car and bought candy. As it started getting dark and we were lost and tired, we knocked on a door and got some adults to help us get home.

We played army in the dirt piles. Scouting over a hill for enemies, I had the first scientific insight I can remember. I realized that in order to see anyone, I had to expose enough of my own head that I'd be visible too. You had to come out of hiding in order to see anything.

Cowboys and Indians, though, was the main game. I loved my cap-gun six-shooters and holsters and neckerchief and cowboy hat. The caps came in matte red rolls, with little disks of black powder set in them. You'd thread the roll inside your metal pistol. When you pulled the trigger, the strip advanced, and the hammer hit the next cap with a bang, and smoke rose. I would like to smell the smacked burnt snap of a detonated cap like that again right now.

There were the fan clubs, or the brotherhoods, of the heroes of the Saturday-morning TV shows. Flash Gordon, who lived in the future and rocketed through outer space. I joined his club. You found out how to join them from the backs of cereal boxes and sent in for a membership card and an ID ring. Sky King, who was a modern-day rancher who flew a little private airplane. Spin and Marty, modern kids at a western boys' camp as presented by *The Mickey Mouse Club*. Zorro and the Cisco Kid and the Lone Ranger. There was often a wandering hero and his devoted sidekick, who provided comic relief. That happened over and over in Howard Hawks and John Ford westerns too. (Whenever I could, I'd take the bus into town on Saturdays to go to a double feature. Often they were John Ford and Howard Hawks movies, by which I was contaminated with the Code of the West.) There were also buddy teams in which the members were equal and were complementary in other ways than as hero and faithful clown. Tonto wasn't a clown with the Lone Ranger, nor was Dean Martin with John Wayne in *Rio Bravo* (Walter Brennan was the clown on that team). The Three Musketeers.

I grew up thinking men worked best in wandering small teams, usually two-man. You needed someone to conspire with, someone to help you maintain the nerve to carry out your ideas. Someone to know what you were thinking (otherwise your thinking didn't really exist). Someone who had qualities you wanted, maybe, too, and that you could acquire to some degree by association.

I remember two things about Pat Thompson, my first best friend. One of those includes the other buddy we would plan a runaway with. At recess in the schoolyard Pat put his arms around our shoulders for a conference and then banged our heads together and laughed. I was shocked he did that. The other is that when Pat moved away the following year, in third grade, we exchanged mementos of each other and what I took was the heel of his shoe. I can still see it in my mind. It's dry and concave with bent little skinny nails poking up from it and his signature on the other side in felt-tipped pen.

In the spring of 1957 Gardenside was still making do with a nineteenth-century one-room schoolhouse for the small children. It stood at the top of an overgrown hill and had been converted to three classrooms, one for each of the first three grades. Down the side of the hill gaped a wide-mouthed shallow cave, where we were to meet at midnight.

All afternoon that day I secretly gathered supplies—crackers and peanut butter and apples—from around the house and smuggled them back to hide under my pillow in the bedroom I shared with my sister. That night I was going to wrap it all in a cloth and tie it to the end of a stick to carry over my shoulder.

The author with his mother and sister, spring 1957.

When bedtime came, and my sister and I had to brush our teeth and get into our pajamas, I couldn't find my damn pajamas. They should have been in the bureau drawer. Then the whole household was helping me look, and just as I realized what I had done my father called out that he had found them along with everything else under my pillow.

It was late but all the lights stayed on. My pretty little sister was awed. And now here is the strange part: my father's reaction. My father told me that at midnight he would drive me to the cave and that if my friends were there I could go with them. I was amazed then and still am now.

Just before midnight we got in the big old Kaiser and rolled the five minutes to the distant rendezvous site. My father was friendly and concerned. My confidence was a little reduced by his careful kindness, but I imagined the triumph of being left with my friends to figure out our next move. They'd think what a great dad I had. We waited in the car with the lights turned off, and nothing happened. No one came. We waited until I couldn't complain that we'd left too soon and then we drove home.

I don't remember anything else about what happened and the only one who remembers it at all is me. My mother doesn't remember that any of it happened; neither does my sister. My father died suddenly of a heart attack some weeks after the runaway plan. The fact that I am the only person from the original night who even remembers that it took place seems poignant, not to mention disturbing, considering its significance to me. My wife teased me about it.

Then I found an old box of papers containing a hand-drawn booklet I'd made for school that year entitled "Runaway Boy," dated November, 1957, a few months after the getaway try. It reads:

This story is true

names have

Been changed

chapter one

My first plans

Well I planed to run away with two school mates named Jack and Clem. We were going to meet at front of school. To live at a place that was next to the school it was a cave. Oh and my name is Jim. One of us was going to bring a blanket one some food one some matches and a candle. We were going to run away because our mother's spanked us to much. I was geting food this is how I did it: I told my mother I wanted a few apples to take out to my friends but I didn't I put it in a hakerchief to keep it together I had a play sword to keep it together. And we were going to meet at 12 o'clock on the dot. I hid the hankercheif under my pillow. Then I went out and played until supper and went to sleep.

Next day I made a sneak tellaphone call to Clem to talk about the runaway and to tell him I might be a little late becuas I live very far away from school. In my hankerchief I had some pajama's you know food I had some old clothes shirt pants shoes. I just couldn't wait for that night but I felt a little unlucky. I went out to play for a little while then came back for supper. I watched t.v. for a little while then I wanted to go to bed I went to get my pajama's but they weren't there you know I told everybody I lost them. Everybody looked I play like I looked to but I didn't. I told them my mother

father and sister not to look under my pillow just a little bit
late. My father looked and there was the hankerchief

Chapter two
A surprise!

I was ashamed that I wanted to runaway. But I still wanted
to. I wanted to run away with Clem and Jack they were my
best friends. But my father said I could runaway! He told
me he would at exactly 12 o'clock he would start the car and
away we would go.

But if Clem and Jack weren't there we would come right
back home. I couldn't wait till midnight but it got here. And
away we went to school. When we got there I told dad to
wait a while because they weren't there!

But they never got there so we went and went to sleep I
dreamed I was a very clean tramp!

THE End

I like how my name in the story, Jim, is a combination of the names
of my two best friends, Jack and Clem.

Kentucky is riddled with caves, and my friends and I would go hunting
for them. We found a few little tunnels tucked away in the surrounding
farmland—openings into the ground that were wet and dark and slick,
where salamanders lived and into which you could squeeze and sit and
then crawl deeper. Their entrances were often signaled in the fields
by clumps of trees that had been left to grow because they filled a dip

in the land that couldn't be plowed. We'd poke around in a crater like that and sometimes in the rubble and undergrowth there would be an entrance. Inside, you'd find that good feeling again that's rare in adulthood, except maybe in drugs and sex, of dreaming and conspiring in a hideout, beyond the pale.

In memories, as in dreams, you often see yourself from outside, as if it were a movie. That's how I remember the morning after my father died, in the summer of 1957.

My sister, Babette, and I slept in beds against opposite walls of our room, which was next to our parents' bedroom, at the back of the house. I see the scene from an angle near, but above, my mother's head, everything dim and out of focus, as she sits on my sister's narrow bed, the one closest to the door, looking down at me beside her. Six-year-old Babette sits on the edge of the bed too, on the other side of me, listening as our mother explains that our father has died during the night. We don't understand the situation very well, though we realize that being dead is supposed to mean he doesn't exist anymore, he is completely gone.

Later in the year, I was embarrassed that the kids in school knew my father had died. I was more conscious of being upset by that than by his actual death, which was just an absence (there wasn't even a funeral).

For a while when I was eight or nine my best friend was a kid named Rusty Roe who lived a few houses down the block. He was a year or two younger than me. I was probably still insecure from my father dying. Rusty's nice father, Chet, who must have been in his late twenties, was an outdoorsman, a hunter and fisherman who subscribed to gun and rod magazines and did taxidermy as a hobby, and who took Rusty and me bass fishing sometimes in a rowboat on a lake.

There were a couple of years there where I got interested in birds. (According to my ma, the very first word I ever spoke was "bird.") I loved walking in the countryside, out past the streets, looking for birds, and I could identify them by song and flight pattern and nest as well as shape and markings. Rusty would go with me, and he knew a lot about them too. We'd carry Peterson's field guides. I collected abandoned nests. I carved birds out of balsa wood and painted them. I bought plastic model kits of birds to glue together and paint.

One early evening, Rusty and I were playing in his backyard when it got time for me to head home, and he misunderstood my leaving as a rejection. He pleaded with me not to go, and started crying, apologizing and begging, and I realized that there was a part of me that liked that he was crying. Something in me was glad to make my friend cry. I hadn't wanted to hurt him, but his tears showed how much he valued me and that I was not the vulnerable one. I got some kind of satisfaction, too, in becoming harder as he got servile. The sudden gulf between us made me want to be alone. It was dusk as I left my friend standing in his storm-fenced back lawn, with its little concrete goldfish pond dug by his father.

While I might be a little nostalgic for the innocence, the grace, that existed before my behavior became consciously calculated, my life was full of pain and fear then, and it wasn't even really innocent either. My nice third-grade teacher, Mrs. Monk, corrected me once because I was acting modest. She advised me not to "fish for compliments." At first I didn't get what she meant, but then I was amazed to realize that it was possible to misunderstand my own behavior, to believe I was doing something for the exact opposite reason I was really doing it.

My flat, vacant, smudged ten-or-eleven-year-old face. There's a panorama or montage of local vistas, the empty suburban hills, shifting slowly behind it, all silent and soft and cold, with visible grain, as I glide around the quiet newly built streets on my bicycle, alone, with no one else in sight. Or I'm sitting in my backyard, suddenly self-aware, or aware that this moment is going to happen again someday, portraying my condition and environment (this sentence on this page in this book).

I probably peaked as a human in the sixth grade. I was golden without conceit. My teacher that year, Mrs. Vicars, made a private special arrangement allowing me to write stories instead of doing the regular homework assignments.

In seventh grade I fell, though, and it would take me years to climb back. The postwar baby boom had caught up with the Lexington school system and it became so overcrowded that a big old wooden jumble downtown was annexed for the exclusive use of hundreds and hundreds of seventh graders from all over the city. As one boy in a large school of unknown kids my age from all over the city, I lost any history and prestige I'd had. I was nobody, and as I wasn't assertive, it was impossible to catch up. All I remember of school that year is my anxiety and unhappiness, mixed with pained envy of the thriving redneck hard-asses: commanding, mature Gary Leach, with his short sleeves folded up his biceps, pegged jeans nonchalantly clinging, short hair waxed in precise furrows, as he murmured consolingly, behind me on the school bus, to the lovely weeping Susan Atkinson beside him, "You can cry on my shoulder"; tough, dashing, chipped-front-toothed Jimmy Gill, Jerry Lee Lewis look-alike; muscular, confident farm boy Hargus Montgomery.

There was one last-minute redeeming experience. Because I was traumatized and couldn't make myself do any homework, my grades had plummeted from effortless excellence to C's and D's and F's. I hadn't attached much importance to grades, but it was mortifying suddenly to be lacking that way. But when the student body was given standardized "achievement tests" at the end of the year I got the highest scores in the whole school. They wouldn't have revealed that to me, but the administration thought I should be talked to, considering my grades. I noticed that teachers all of a sudden acted differently towards me. I was glamorous. They'd stop and look at me as I walked by.

All those years of junior high school—seventh through ninth grade— were awful. Because of the overcrowding I attended a different school each year, with my classmates always changing and unknown. I couldn't bring myself to do homework. I had insomnia too, because I was anxious about being unprepared and being such a failure and disliking everything. I would put off the homework, even the most important, until the night before it was due, and then stay up in misery, sweating in my new attic bed among any texts I might paraphrase to patch together and pad a fake paper. The insomnia was like being paralyzed in a spotlight, like being trapped. I knew it was my anxiety about doing badly and about losing status that kept me awake, but I still couldn't force myself to do the stupid homework or truly figure out what was going on, and all this would amplify itself, like feedback in my head, but it was duller than that. More like crawling skin. Like there was some drug I needed that I didn't have.

I hated the raw oppression of being a kid once I became self-aware. I don't like "alpha" people as a rule, and in the random enclosed societies of schools, you have to deal with them. I didn't like being stuck with strangers, period, either. I also didn't like being told what to do, and of course school and childhood itself is about the authority of all grown-ups. I knew as well as any of them what was worthwhile, but because I was a kid and they were bigger and had more power than me, I was cheated.

I remember making some promises to my adult self when I was still a kid—or extracting some promises from my adult self. I promised not to forget how arbitrary and unfair adult rules are. I promised to remain true to the principles I grasped that adults sometimes pretended to know but hardly ever behaved in accordance with.

I wanted to have a life of adventure. I didn't want anybody telling me what to do. I knew this was the most important thing and that all would be lost if I pretended otherwise like grown-ups did.

Those monstrous, boxlike, snouted, yolk-colored school buses, with their rotten black lettering, symbolized loneliness and humiliation. The weather they rolled through was gray and rainy and I gazed out the window hoping not to be noticed, except by a particular girl.

CHAPTER TWO

Yesterday there was a pretty girl sitting in front of my wife and me at a movie and most of the time all I could see of her was her hair. When I sat behind girls in classrooms in grade school, their hair could drive me crazy. It wasn't even actually alive, but it was more affecting than most people's faces because of the intimate way it was involved with the girl it belonged to. It was out of my reach while being right there, completely exposed, with all its uncontrolled, feral implications mixed with the messages of its grooming, and all of that heartrendingly moving for the way its possessor was innocent of the effects. It was like spying on someone sleeping.

In third grade I was crazy about Mimi McClellan. If I try to picture her, there's no face. There's just her dirty-blond hair in a big bouffant. But no one that young would have worn a bouffant like that, when I think about it. And it was 1958 and people didn't wear that hairdo until Jackie Kennedy showed up two or three years later. I would lie in my bed at night thinking of Mimi McClellan and fantasize getting hit by a car so that she would take my hand and I could tell her that I loved her.

In the sixth grade there was Janet Adelstein. It is probably Janet's hair I put on Mimi. Because Janet did have a big dark-blond bouffant, preserved by hair spray: a silken mist, a soft fragrant mesh of crystallization.

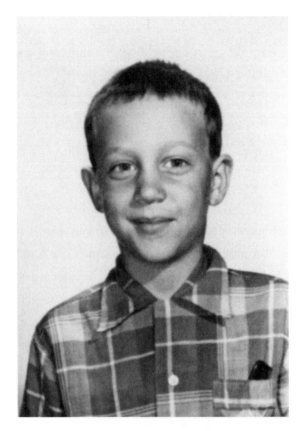

crazy about Mimi McClellan

The young girls wore white cotton blouses with ring-neck collars, and cardigans and culottes. Maybe a delicate gold-chain necklace, and tennis shoes or Bass loafers and bobby socks. Many of the girls had breasts by then. Janet's were larger than most.

I never revealed my feelings to her either. A year or two later we chanced on each other somewhere and we talked and it turned out she'd had a crush on me at that same time. That seemed tragic, Shakespearean.

I can't remember when I started masturbating, but it was long before I could come. We boys thought there was something perverse and inferior about jacking off. Having sex alone. I had this tactic for excusing it where I wouldn't start until I could give myself a hard-on without actually touching my penis, but just by thinking. Considering those fantasies now, I wish I could see them as if they were movies—I was so ignorant about sex, it would be cool to see what I was picturing (I know Roy Baker's mother sometimes figured in them).

There was a great *Mad* magazine spread in the sixties that featured photos of 3-D versions of children's drawings—photos of everyday objects constructed as if the children's drawings of them were accurate, such as a stubby little airplane with different-length wings that pointed in different directions, and propellers on it that looked like broken matchsticks, and dripping misspelled words on its fuselage.

Human works that don't hide the crudity of the approximate nature of their representation are the best.

At the same time, the little I did know about the mechanics of sexual activity when I was thirteen was plenty. Drawing a picture no more detailed than an infinity sign with a dot in the middle of each loop of it, and below that the outline of an hourglass that had a downward-pointing triangle of scribble in the bottom center of it, was enough to give a boy a giant erection. I spent half the eighth grade having to walk with my schoolbooks held in front of my jeans to hide the sideways bulge. Sometimes a few drops of liquid would escape just from the friction of the fabric and once or twice it then actually shuddered into spurts right there in the crowded corridor.

When I eventually got a finger inside a vagina, at thirteen or fourteen, it was like being ordained into a new dimension, almost supernatural, as if I had pulled the sword from the stone. I went for a long walk afterwards, furtively passing my fingers under my nose every few hundred yards, the scent insignia of my kingdom.

I didn't have full sexual intercourse until I was fifteen. My only interest in her was that I thought she might let me do that. Sex drive overcomes almost everything. Many have died behind their dicks. After all, where does reckless aggression come from but testosterone, and where does testosterone come from? Many have died and many around them have been totally fucked. And often greatly liked it. But this unlucky girl didn't like it, or very much of anything else, as far as I could tell. She was a waitress at a Big Boy drive-in by the university. She was nineteen, and a hillbilly from Appalachia, and she was not just narrow-minded and ignorant, but dumb as a rock and about as energetic. I flirted with her when I'd go in for a hamburger. I told her I was a premed student. I walked her home from work. Soon she gave me the key to her apartment.

The making out was not relaxed. It was like hacking through wilderness brush that clung to your ankles and scratched your face, as you struggled on, further and further, your heart racing because the incentive was so powerful. Namely female genitals: dripping wet pussy. In the end, her pussy wasn't even very wet, she was so nervous and put-upon. Fucking her was horrible, though God knows I couldn't get enough. Even once her clothes were off and she was lying under me on the bed, she didn't participate, but resisted uncomfortably and for appearance's sake, all the way through full penetration, which she refrained from giving any sign of joining, but rather lay there stoically, performing only a last symbolic hip buck or two of denial and refusal. This was to confirm that she wasn't a disgusting person, but was permitting this terrible, embarrassing act as a begrudged extreme favor to me.

I understand there still are cultural strata where this is standard behavior even among married people. Thank god for pornography. Thank god for the sexual revolution and the pill, and rebellious, fun-loving girls. Though I can't deny I am still repressed and American enough to like sex dirty. And I do love hair. Because it's dead but personal and because I'm moved by the futility of its attempts to warm and protect the places where it grows.

CHAPTER THREE

A s clumsy and alien as I was after the age of twelve, I was still a romantic hero inside, and I couldn't help wanting to force a reconciliation between the inner and outer, even if the result was grotesque. Sometimes as a kid I would fantasize a life as an obese bedridden recluse, managing the whole world like a spider in its web, sensitive to every tremor, instantly responding. A kind of prodigal Orson Welles or crazy Howard Hughes, haunted Superman. I believed I was mesmerizing and charming but wisely feared testing that socially.

I started getting into low-grade scrapes with the authorities in the ninth grade. One morning I used ingredients from an old home-chemistry set to rig an explosion on my school bus. It was only noise and smoke, but I liked it. I was suspended for two or three days for that.

Later in the year I set up a cigarette slow fuse on a pack of firecrackers in a locker at school. The rapid popping was amplified into one long crashing boom by the metal box. My homeroom teacher leaped into the hall and jumped back gasping, "The clock exploded!" . . . I couldn't stop laughing, which might have been what gave me away. I was suspended for a week that time.

Then, out of nowhere, for the tenth grade I got a scholarship to the private school in town. My seventh-grade biology teacher had gotten a job there, and the school, Sayre, had started a two-student scholarship program. Mr. Bailey sold them on me, and my mother got a phone call offering full tuition.

Larry Flynn, the other scholarship student, became my best friend. His scholarship was weighted towards athletics, mine academics. He ended up the quarterback of the ragtag football team and the star guard in basketball, while my grades stayed bad, but we both liked our situations. The rich girls were inspiring. That slim sweet-smelling pale freckled flesh swaddled in cashmere and combed Egyptian cotton. The public school girls were rawer and in some ways sexier, but they were harder to figure out, for the likes of me. (In the eighth grade when I had my very first chance to have sex with a girl—a typical poor working-class kid from school, and a virgin like me—I didn't go through with it because it seemed to be hurting her too much. She quickly found herself a less sensitive guy.) I was happier at a school as small as Sayre where everybody got to know everybody.

I continued to get in trouble, though. In those days people often left their keys in their cars. In my neighborhood you could always find a car with keys in its ignition inside forty-five minutes. I took them for joyrides with friends, trying to learn how to drive in the process, planning to return them before they were missed. I'd sneak out at night and take my ma's or friends' parents' cars too. I guess I was more reckless with those. I was caught in them twice. First, when I lifted the keys to my ma's.

After taking forever to tiptoe in slow motion down the creaky stairs from my bedroom after bedtime, it was out the front door into a huge night that was brighter than the inside because of the moon and stars, while chilled, the sparkling gray grass and car wet with condensation. Friends met me in the yard and we put the car in neutral and pushed it

From Sayre basketball team, 1965.
Left to right: Richard Meyers, Larry Flynn.

out of the driveway and rolled it partway down the hill before switching on the engine and driving off.

We decided to go to Cincinnati, ninety miles north. Taking the four-lane interstate was like shooting at seventy-five miles an hour down the aisle of a giant empty supermarket, big signs listing options whizzing up the windshield. We laughed and drank and smoked. The secret risk we might crash was a buzz too. I most definitely wasn't in complete control. Once we got to Cincinnati, nobody knew anywhere to go so we turned around.

Back in Lexington, we decided to explore the black neighborhood under the viaduct, and I got lost in the badly lit half-paved streets, and, trying to maneuver out of a dead end, rammed into a pole and killed the motor. When I restarted, the car backfired and weirdly began accelerating uncontrollably. In a minute we were speeding out of control through the middle of town. I was afraid to use the brakes because I thought it might totally fuck the car to do that while it was getting gas. So I switched off the ignition while going full speed. As we coasted to a reasonable velocity I restarted the engine, which made the car backfire again and resume increasing throttle. Pretty soon this ongoing stop-and-start drag-race backfire routine got the attention of the police, and two or three patrol cars appeared in pursuit. After a half mile or so, I braked and we jumped out and ran. They chased us with dogs and hauled us in.

The other incident involved Leslie Woolfolk. She was a cynical, pale beanpole of a girl who ran with a set of voluntarily outcast girls from Sayre who mocked everything. They were like a skittish herd of scaled-down giraffes with pretty, flat kitty-cat faces. I liked all of them.

She agreed to meet me at midnight with her parents' car keys. We were going to drive into the country out by Versailles, where another of the giraffe girls lived on a horse farm. Her parents' car had a manual transmission, though, and that was new to me. We managed to reach the farmland, but as I was backing out of a wrong dark driveway, I overshot and got us hopelessly stuck in a ditch.

We spent the cold night in a hay shack, using each other's body heat for warmth, despite the frustrating limitations she put on it. We figured that in the morning we'd flag a tractor tow and then escape to Florida. At dawn, back in the car, a trooper tapped on our window.

The school threatened expulsion. I didn't understand that, since it didn't seem like a school matter. Anyway, our kind schoolmates protested with a petition and the headmaster relented. We were both suspended for two weeks.

My ma's solution to the suspension dilemma this time was to make me paint the exterior woodwork on our house—the window frames and door frames and the panels under the gutters. She let me listen to music while I did it though. I had a little portable record player I could run out to the yard on an extension cord. I only owned three LPs: *The Rolling Stones, Now!; Bringing It All Back Home* by Bob Dylan; and *Kinks-Size* ("featuring 'All Day and All of the Night' and 'Tired of Waiting for You'") by the Kinks. I played them over and over as I stood up on the ladder painting in the sun. The Stones record started to melt and warp. That night I put it in a hot oven between two frying pans and the next day it sounded even better.

It seems unlikely, but seven or eight years later when I started having a band myself, those three records, the first I ever owned, and the only ones I owned for some time, still held true as what excited me in music—for being fast, aggressive, and scornful, but complicated and full of feelings. They were just casual soundtrack pastimes in 1965; they didn't mean much more to me than what shirt a person might wear or what stranger might sit next to me on the bus to town. Sure, if I had thought about it when I was listening to them, I would've said I wanted the life I imagined the boys who made those records must have had, but I took the music for granted. The music was everything I wanted—it filled me with confidence and restlessness and the feeling of having inside information and sex appeal, but I took it for granted. And I believed I could do it myself under the right circumstances. Though I never expected to actually try to do it myself. I knew from experience that practicing a musical instrument was boring (I'd had clarinet lessons for a year or so), and it seemed very unlikely, inconceivable in fact, that someone I knew (namely me) would get to make records.

CHAPTER FOUR

One day, in the shadow of my teenage misadventures, my mother drove me in silence through traffic towards a shopping center. I was sitting against the passenger door in the big front seat of the '55 Buick that had replaced the Kaiser. Without a word, she pulled onto the shoulder of the road, stopped the car, and proceeded to beat her head rhythmically but violently against the steering wheel. Blood appeared on her forehead. I wondered how I should behave in the situation.

It was probably my final Lexington mishap that led to the head beating. Rebecca, the Big Boy's waitress, whom I'd been seeing all that summer I was fifteen, had come home early from work one night and caught me drinking in her apartment with a couple of other girls. Her revenge was to call my mother and claim that she was pregnant by me. She also called the head of the English department at the university where my mom was studying.

Just at this same time though, in 1965, my ma completed her PhD and found a job teaching American literature at Old Dominion, a state college in Norfolk, Virginia. We drove there in our first brand-new car, a little red Chevy Corvair that was Uncle Dick's and Aunt Phyllis's graduation gift to her. We moved into an apartment converted from the second floor of an old two-story house on a corner of Jamestown Crescent, which was the main avenue of a quiet, tree-shaded, twenties-era residential neighborhood called Larchmont, a three-minute drive from the college.

Norfolk was a nowhere place. It made Lexington look elegant. Its heart was an enormous naval base, the world's largest, and the rest of the town matched it in steel and concrete dreariness, every location linked by little tunnels and bridges across a network of polluted bays and waterways. There were a few brick vestiges of an old Virginia that was at least as conservative as the anonymous military, but even the Atlantic shore, twenty miles away at Virginia Beach, which is really what attracted my mother to the job, was ugly: a seedy wad of pretentious middle-class or grungy cheap hotels surrounded by advertising signs, T-shirt-and-souvenir shops, fast food, and blocks and blocks of nondescript small beach houses.

I was enrolled for the eleventh grade at a massive public high school. I'd never been able to study, and now I would be subhuman socially again, too. I would much rather have had a room alone in a cheap boardinghouse anywhere in the U.S. than carry schoolbooks around those wretched halls.

Ma, after a few weeks of my miserable threats and promises, agreed to look for a school more like Sayre. My history was a problem—not only the suspensions, but even at Sayre on scholarship my grades had been all D's and C's. We didn't have any money. My mother talked the situation over with Grandma Linda and they did some research and turned up a coed boarding school in Delaware that would accept me. My grandma gave my mom most of the tuition.

Sanford Preparatory School was about eight miles northwest of Wilmington, clustered in 185 acres of fields and wooded hills. Most of the 165 students across the school's six grades lived at the school. Some of the five or six small sex-segregated dorms were converted old farm structures, others more recent generic quasi-barracks. The classroom buildings were former farmhouses mostly, and there was an angular, modern new library, walled in big panes of glass that made it cozy inside on snowy days. The school had a brand-new "fieldhouse" (gym), as well as tennis courts, and hockey, baseball, football, and lacrosse fields, and even a small stable. The boys wore sports coats—school blazer optional—and ties, and the girls knee socks and kilts and, over their white cotton blouses, blazers or cardigans.

It was a similar environment to Sayre. My work habits didn't change. By February I was on academic probation, with an F in Advanced Math, a D in Spanish, and a C in English. I considered the bad marks a problem, but not a big one—it'd been like this since the seventh grade. The ease of the life was becoming a little disturbing though. My role at the school was that of the skeptic and troublemaker and joker, the guy who didn't take any of it seriously and was always looking for illicit adventure. That was pretty close to how I felt inside, but I needed to bust out of the frame, including busting out of the frame of the frame.

In the spring a friend and I snuck out of the dorm one night and broke into the school clinic and stole a couple of quarts of cherry-flavored codeine cough syrup from a five-gallon jug. I would drink a plastic cup of it in the morning and then goof and navigate in the nod, my head on my arms in the back of class, for an hour or two at the start of the school day.

I remember rainy weather with the *Aftermath* LP by the Rolling Stones playing in someone's room off the common area in my dormitory. "Stupid Girl," "Under My Thumb," "I Am Waiting." The record was so

stole a couple of quarts of cherry-flavored codeine cough syrup

ragged and tinselly and expert and full of personality—cavernous and wiseass. The Rolling Stones came up with good titles too. *Aftermath.* Who would have guessed that that word had the gore, the avalanche feeling it does? It seems like an innocuous word, but no—isolated, it's ominous, and it's about achievement, not an aspiration but an accomplishment, specifically a serious crime or other disaster. It's mass killings and terrible deceptions that have aftermaths.

I didn't buy into the mythology of rock and roll bands though. As I said, the music was just a common feature of the environment. I wasn't a "fan." The style of some of the groups was exciting, but the musicians were people who had taken a chance direction into music. (I still prefer that angle on it, the way it is when a band starts out.) Half the beauty of rock and roll is that "anyone can do it" in the sense that it's not about being a virtuoso but about just being plugged in in a certain way, just having an innocent instinct and a lot of luck. That's why it's the art of teenagers. There wasn't anything awe-inspiring or even especially interesting to me about bands. (It's only since I've had a fair amount of firsthand contact with pop musicians that I've come to see that they actually are, or, more precisely, have become, a breed apart. I'm still not susceptible to the fascination with them, but "sacred monster" is definitely the job description, at least for the front person, the singer in a band. Being a pop star, a front person, takes indestructible certainty of one's own irresistibility. That's the monster part. If that ego confidence doesn't eventually come so naturally that living at all is to flaunt it, you won't have what's necessary to give your audience the show, the stimulation, it needs. The audience needs it from the performer in order to identify with it, to give themselves the sense of their own power, to get the full effect and function of rock and roll. It starts off natural and even cute, in the beginners, but is fed and tested on the way to stardom until it's grotesque in every dimension except that of performance, where it is thrilling and uplifting, which is the sacred part. It's also usually a monster of stress on its adepts; not really a fate to be desired. Which is another reason the stars are so cranky. They hate everyone for making them into what they've turned out to be, so they rub everyone's faces in it.)

In the summer of 1966, after my first year at Sanford, I was punished for my bad showing by being sent to stay with my mother's mother, Mama Doll, in Sherman, Texas, where she was a clerk at an air force base. I was made to spend the desert days seated on an upended oilcan crate in front of a gas station, waiting to jockey fuel pumps. A few times a week I had remedial Spanish lessons. I was squirming in the fantastic crush I had on my young Spanish tutor. On top of all that, or underneath it, I suffered a hemorrhoid, though I didn't know what it was. I could have guessed it was something that ugly sounding, but, being too embarrassed to ask anybody about it, I ended up trying to slice it away myself with a razor blade, in the stained bathroom of the dusty, dark, junk-filled old house where Mama Doll lived with her adored parakeet.

By the time I returned to Sanford in the fall, *Life* magazine had brought to the hinterlands stories of long-haired kids with their flowers and beads and psychedelic drugs. A simple Beatles bowl haircut was still extreme in rural Delaware. Once or twice students were rumored to have smoked a joint on campus, but that was dubious hearsay. Most of our knowledge of drugs still came from the beat writers. Their drug use seemed exotic and sexy, even though their jazz-and-poetry-loving Zen party world had seeped through deeply enough that a whole class of people you had some acquaintance with more or less lived it. That dilution undermined the seriousness with which you could take it. I couldn't respond wholeheartedly to the beat writers because there was that ubiquitous youth group who considered pocket copies of *Howl* to be a secret handshake and I didn't want any part of that. I was suspicious of the mystic dogma too, the insistence on spontaneity. I'll be spontaneous when I feel like it.

I liked drugs though. I liked the instant getaway and the physical pleasure of both narcotics and then psychedelics, and, later, stimulants. I never did a ton of psychedelic drugs, but I started relatively early. I was the first person I knew who did any. I used some at Sanford in that first month of the twelfth grade.

I'd read in a magazine that certain morning glory seeds were hallucinogenic. They were easy to use. You only had to wash them and then grind them up. You needed a few seed packets' worth, and they tasted bad, so you had to mix the powder with peanut butter or something, but that was all there was to it. So, late one afternoon I forced back a few packets of Heavenly Blues. It may have been the happiest day of my teenage years up until then.

I was walking up the path towards my dormitory when I felt the drugs kick in—waves of almost sexual pleasure that also felt like power, and heightened naked perception. It was as if the drugs dissolved all the filters so that everything got perceptible, and everything perceptible important. The classic cliché image of a person under the influence of psychedelics is the drug taker gazing at his hand as he waves it around in front of his face. What's happening is that he's seeing trails, like comet tails of flowing stop-motion sown in the air by his fingers. They're not put there by the drug. If you swish your hands around in front of your face right now you'll see the same thing. It's just that you don't usually notice it because it's not useful to notice. On psychedelic drugs you notice it; you notice everything. It was like I'd stepped from a more demanding dimension, for which I was suited by having correspondingly greater abilities, like Superman on Krypton, into this earthly one where my capabilities became superpowers.

A few guys knew what I'd done and the news spread around the dormitory. It was hard for me to talk because all the words sounded wrong and too final. There was also that drunken effect of feeling free not just because I couldn't help doing what I was doing, but because I was aware that because I was fucked up I wouldn't be responsible for whatever I did.

Dormmates surrounded me in my room, trying to protect me from getting into trouble. I sat on the edge of the lower bunk and then stood and started for the door and they blocked me. I tried to push through them and they wrestled me back. I'd keep to myself, sitting quietly, and wait, as they chatted, until they let their guard down, and then I'd rush the door. It was funny, like something in a cartoon. After a while of this we were making too much commotion and they had to let me out.

There was a school dance going on. Students and a few faculty supervisors filled a big second-story room in one of the older buildings. The light was low and there were crepe paper streamers taped up, and a record was playing.

The upper school had a mascot geek, a sophomore flattered by the attention he got from upperclassmen who circled him to suggest he do humiliating things, like play with himself. I was standing off to one side of the room and I happened to notice him on the dance floor in the crowd. He was in love with cheerleader Marilyn Talbert, a dark-haired, skinny, demure fifteen-year-old with sad, bright eyes and gem-cut cupid's-bow lips that smiled lopsidedly. I saw him shuffling across the floor. Marilyn Talbert and I were probably the only two people in the room aware of him. He was approaching her, and when he got there he asked her to dance. She said no. I started crying.

At breakfast in the cafeteria the next morning I was tired and disoriented but I wasn't tripping anymore. As I moved along the line at the steam tables I felt all eyes on me. But despite my sleepy spaciness and self-consciousness, I felt free, cut loose. Something wasn't over, and there would be collateral repercussions, but I wasn't worried about them; I was just curious, even eager in a subdued kind of way. I felt good.

Later in the day, I was called to the offices of the headmaster and threatened with expulsion. I tried to cast the drug-taking as scientific investigation. I'm not sure how effective that was, but they didn't expel me; I was suspended for a week again.

When I returned from the suspension, it was the week of my seventeenth birthday. School was anticlimactic. I was itchy and didn't care about school at all anymore.

I'd become close friends that fall with a guy I'd only known a little bit the previous year, Tom Miller. The thing that brought us together at school, and would keep us together for most of the coming seven or eight years, was as negative as it was positive. We were both inner-oriented people who didn't respect much convention and who felt apart from others. We also shared tastes for certain kinds of writing and music and shared an anti-real humor.

Tom was a wild card at Sanford. First, he was a day student, not a boarder, so he was less well-known. He was quiet and tense, but he made a lot of ghostly jokes. Most of the world seemed incomprehensibly

From Sanford Preparatory yearbook, 1966. *Top row, third from left:* Tom Miller; *fourth from left:* Richard Meyers.

weird to him, and he was susceptible to all kinds of irrational explanations for that, from things like flying saucers, to extreme conspiracy theories, to obscure religious mysticism. He knew that these beliefs, or suspicions, would seem crazy to a lot of people, and that was part of why he was so private.

He was a high-strung person who didn't know how to communicate socially except on his own narrow terms and in his personal language or style, though in those days he was more easygoing and gregarious and mildly whimsical than he'd eventually become.

He had a great sensibility. I can't remember for sure how far along it had gotten in twelfth grade, but by the time we were reunited in New York a couple of years later, he liked free jazz like Albert Ayler and Eric Dolphy and poetry that resembled it, like Kerouac's *Mexico City Blues*, in its disregard for boundaries and its spontaneity and desperation and spiritual desire and humor. He liked obsessive outsiders—artists whose works were made along patterns you could feel were viscerally, materially connected to the true wacky or hidden reality, because the works were made of the mind substance of people who couldn't help themselves, because they were driven to create, even if unskilled by orthodox standards. And he liked the other side of that coin, namely highly gifted, hardworking, fully self-aware and sophisticated, worldly artists who nevertheless didn't give a fuck about pleasing anyone or taking anything too seriously, and who were naturally subversive, and, in their own kind of purity, were incapable of doing bad work—like, in music, say, the original Sun Records musicians, or Link Wray, or pop artists just that wild, like the Rolling Stones in some of their earlier self-written singles, or Bob Dylan. And always there was the funniness of everything, or of everything that was interesting.

When I got back to school, things just didn't seem right. It was a moment when choosing to go a certain direction was almost an aesthetic decision. How could I resume school? It would ruin the future memory. I didn't realize this for a few days though. It came like an inspiration that had been rising below the surface, the way it might dawn on a trained animal that it could actually just leave the yard.

"Let's take off," I said. Tom agreed.

We thought we'd head south. We had enough pocket money to get train tickets to DC, and then we could begin hitchhiking.

CHAPTER FIVE

W e were heading for Florida. We didn't know anybody there, or know anything about the place except that it was warm and airy, and there was plenty of citrus fruit and seafood, and girls who smelled like suntan lotion and had little particles of sand on them here and there, including inside the waistbands of their panties. We would be fugitive poets they'd care for.

Those days on the road, escaped from school with Tom, gave me the strongest dose yet of my favorite feeling: of leaving myself behind for another world. There are a lot of ways to get that feeling. A drug can do it; so can a new type of work, or falling in love, or just changing your appearance; but actually taking off and abandoning all your previous identity's responsibilities and history and relationships is probably the most pure and exhilarating.

There's one simple, seemingly innocuous experience that's emblematic of that 1966 school runaway for me, an experience that was new and was enabled by our escape: simply to sit in a diner in the darkest depths of the night drinking coffee with a friend. For many years it kept its potency, and for most of those years that friend was Tom. There's an eternal, godlike feeling to sitting with a good friend in the middle of the night, speaking low and laughing, lazily ricocheting around in each other's minds, eyes a little fuzzy and stinging maybe, sipping the flavorful, stimulating sugary hot milky coffee, voices hoarse, the restaurant's harsh light isolating you inside the rampant darkness beyond the windows.

I don't know if I can quite get back to our states of consciousness to describe the pleasure of those days after we took off from school. In one sense they provided a template for the future, but in another way they're irretrievable. We were sixteen and seventeen (Tom wouldn't turn seventeen until December—I was almost three months older), and we were tall and skinny and gawky, with our wrists always poking out of our sleeves. Everything was a lark, and also a tentative exploration, since so much we were doing we were doing for the first time. We were always looking for laughs, and our egos were undeveloped, so we could laugh at each other and ourselves almost without limit and hardly any behavior was out of bounds. We liked to act like idiots, we sincerely identified with bums on the street, and we were drunk with our new freedom.

For some reason we brought out a sense of ridiculousness in each other at the same time that we felt like artists, like people living in order to plumb life and to get by on our wits. But it was a crime to take anything too seriously, as oppressed as we felt by the adult and conventional world. All the most serious art is not only sad but hilarious. What other intelligent way to live is there but to laugh about it? The alternative, also respectable, is suicide. But how could you do that? Not only would it betray a woeful lack of humor, but it would keep you from finding out what was going to happen next.

We hardly stopped in DC but took off hitchhiking from there. I'd contacted some Sayre friends to say I'd be slipping through Lexington, and one of them offered a vacant little farmhouse out in a vegetable field near town where Tom and I could stay for a few days. It was furnished but there was no phone or utilities or food, and of course we didn't have a car. At one point, we had nothing to eat but the raw corn and beans we could scavenge from the crop rows. But we were treated like heroes when my friends came by.

Just before we left, they threw us a party, and, during it, I finally got to have two-person sex again. I barely knew the girl, but she was pretty and we both got drunk. It felt like how it must be for a soldier going off to war, or a rock star who deserves love for his type of noble sacrifice. We got the only bedroom to ourselves while people were drinking and shouting in the other rooms. It was dark in the bedroom, but I was so greedy that I asked her to let me look between her naked legs with a flashlight and she agreed, the goddess.

Tom and I started hitchhiking south again. Soon we'd made it pretty far, to southeastern Alabama, only a short distance from Florida. It was cold there in the middle of the October night. We stood along a two-lane road that wound through the fields and piney woods. Traffic was sparse but twice cars had slowed and pulled over just in order to speed off as we ran up, redneck kids hooting at us. We decided to wait out the dark down in the stubble of harvested crops beyond the road. We gathered brush and twigs and branches and made a little campfire.

We got giddy, cursing the natives and provoking each other, and started flinging burning sticks around the field. We hadn't particularly intended it but pretty soon a few patches here and there caught fire. We levitated in our power. I don't know what we might have done next, but suddenly we were surrounded by the police. There was a fire truck too, and the cops had dogs. We claimed to be Florida college kids but there was an alert out for the missing schoolboys. They arrested and jailed us and called our parents.

We'd been gone about two weeks. At home, it turned out that this time the school wouldn't keep me; we were expelled.

Tom decided to continue in public school in Wilmington, but I couldn't turn back. I needed to make my own life. I realized that the most fertile site for that was New York City, but I was a minor and my mother reminded me she could call the police if I left. I didn't think she would call the police, but I proposed a deal—I'd agree to attend the awful Norfolk high school until I could earn $100 as a stake for myself, if she wouldn't report me when I left. (In 1966, $100 was worth about $700 in 2012 money.) The federal minimum wage back then was $1.25 an hour—so, working part-time after school, it would take me weeks to earn the money. I knew she thought that because I was irresponsible and lazy I wouldn't be able to hold a job that long, or even that I wouldn't have the persistence to find one. She finally had to concede the terms, and I found a job right away working after school in a storefront newsstand downtown that specialized in porn.

School was a joke. In English class we were being taught the forms of correspondence we might need to know to take our places in society. When we were assigned to write a sample birthday-present thank-you note, mine read:

November 18, 1966

Dear Betty,

Thank you very much for your thoughtful gift, *The Wit of De Sade*. Our entire family laughed aloud at the rollicking humor of the "merry marquis."

No one came to my birthday party, but I had a great deal

of fun blowing out the candles after I lit them.

Thanks again for the delightful book.

Gratefully yours,

Richard

For the sample job-application letter I sought a position as defecator in a fertilizer factory.

After school I was reading Dylan Thomas. For years, later, I was embarrassed to admit he'd inspired me. He was so overwrought and "poetic," his language all biblical and astronomical and anatomical (saviors, radium, sun, tongues, fountains, nerve, bone), and concerned with big dramatic subjects, even if the poems didn't really make intellectual sense but were more like music. Whereas the New York poets I eventually came to love were wiseass goofs and collaging phraseologists, adorers of everyday details, never taking themselves too seriously.

I basically haven't read Thomas since I was eighteen. But now when I randomly open his *Collected Poems* and find:

> To-day, this insect, and the world I breathe,
> Now that my symbols have outelbowed space,
> Time at the city spectacles, and half
> The dear, daft time I take to nudge the sentence,
> In trust and tale I have divided sense,
> Slapped down the guillotine, the blood-red double
> Of head and tail made witnesses to this
> Murder of Eden and green genesis.

. . . I have to say it gives me a kick and I can detect in myself that seventeen-year-old's reaction to it of wanting to see what I could do in little word compartments on the page like that. ("Now that my symbols have outelbowed space"—Oh yeah! *Really.*) I can't remember what led me to Thomas, but I was always reading and had always gotten a lot of mileage out of words, incoming and outgoing, and he was a notorious icon of the kind of life I imagined for myself: a guy who spun himself out of his head into women's beds and headlines and a general orgiastic existence, living by his wits, without going to school and working a job, and left a trail of songs of it, pretty songs of thanks and praise and tears and nonsense, souvenirs of his discoveries and losses, for everyone to enjoy and ponder and live with him. When I got tired of that poetry it was because it came to seem like overblown mystification and drama, like fog machines at a rock concert, taking what was probably only a vague little idea or quasi-insight per poem and decorating and declaiming it, Robert Plant style, not with the mystery of being too profound for clear words, but rather the vagueness and insubstantiality of the original idea being further distanced and obscured by preacherly howling and growling.

But when I look at it now I get off on it, and can actually read it as direct in its own way, and get that that's actually a lot of the pleasure of it. If you read that stanza as if it were straight speech, it's a weird funhouse that keeps surprising you with the turns it takes and the scenes that pass and the jumps it makes between levels. It's crude too, jamming together unmatching phrases, and in that way it's lovably unpretentious. It could almost be a cutup. And, after all, my main man New York poet Ted Berrigan himself in *The Sonnets* repeatedly used an allusion to Thomas: "Shall it be male or female in the tub?" (The Thomas poem "If I Were Tickled by the Rub of Love" twice asks, "Shall it be male or female?" and then goes "rub" repeatedly.) In fact, the style of Berrigan's *Sonnets* is not that far from Thomas. Take just the same number of lines as in the above stanza from the start of the first poem in *The Sonnets* ("I"):

> His piercing pince-nez. Some dim frieze
> Hands point to a dim frieze, in the dark night.
> In the book of his music the corners have straightened:
> Which owe their presence to our sleeping hands.
> The ox-blood from the hands which play
> For fire for warmth for hands for growth
> Is there room in the room that you room in?
> Upon his structured tomb:

I'd fallen for Thomas's poetry and I got his book of letters, too, and a biography. He looked like a dignified piglet with a cigarette butt stuck in his lips, and his messy curls, and a sloppy bow tie. You could see how it took a lot of attitude to make his bulbous visage as sexy as he managed to do, and it also took a lot of liquor and a good sense of humor, along with his way with words.

I went to the library too, to see who the other modern poets were. I disliked the educated, fastidious, grim ones like, say, Robert Lowell. I discovered William Carlos Williams, and that decided me that poetry was the ticket. He'd had book after handsome book published by New Directions, and was treated like a VIP, and I knew I could write better than him. I thought if he could make it with a few white chickens, a wet red wheelbarrow, and some cold plums in the icebox, I could sure damn well make it too. Dylan Thomas was my model, but it was Williams who actually sold me on my vocation. Funny, even though I never did develop much interest in Williams, those objects of his are the highlights of this paragraph, no question. Objectivism they called it.

CHAPTER SIX

A day after Christmas in 1966 I left home permanently on a bus to New York.

Four or five Sanford boys were in the city for the holidays. I shared a hotel room off Washington Square Park with a couple of them and we bought some bad street grass and did some drinking, and then, when they returned to school, I was alone again and almost broke.

I checked the classifieds for a job and the next day I was working as a stock boy at Macy's. A young Puerto Rican coworker with a big Afro agreed to take me as a roommate. I moved out of my cheap hotel and into his tiny furnished single room at 1 Irving Place, on the corner of Fourteenth Street. There was a bed and closet, a little table, and a sink. The bathroom was in the hall. The rent was about $20 a week, which we split.

We lived above a Horn and Hardart automat—a cafeteria where you could also buy pie slices and macaroni and deep-fried fish fillets from little windows in the wall, like fancy coin-operated post office boxes that contained food. The busboy service was minimal, so we would fill up by taking a table that had just been vacated and eating whatever was left on it.

My roommate called himself a classical composer and he had some creased blank music sheets that he would sometimes sit and stare at, every once in a while penciling some notes on the staffs. He drank a lot. We had to share the bed and he would come back drunk in the middle of the night and get in bed and throw up. It was a little operetta of its own.

After a few months I'd saved up enough to get myself an apartment. From then on I quit jobs and changed apartments continuously. Both were so plentiful there was no reason to keep a job if I'd saved enough to go for two weeks without working, and there was no reason to pay rent if my income got too low, since it took a couple of months of non-payment before the landlord could legally evict me. All of my apartments were small and most of them were dark and some were mildly dangerous. I can remember seven of them from 1967 through 1975, and I remember working that first year as: the Macy's stock boy, a door-to-door magazine subscription salesman, a stock clerk in a bookstore, and a book fetcher and shelver at the main branch of the New York Public Library on Fifth Avenue at Forty-Second Street, and I'm sure there were more. Later I'd drive taxis, get a lot of unskilled office work on assignments from temp agencies, sort mail in the post office, unload fruit and vegetable crates in shape-up crews down at the docks all night, and carry fifty-pound cement bags up to tenement roofs as a construction worker.

In the course of that construction job Allen Ginsberg once liked my looks on the street and invited me over. It made me think of Walt Whitman admiring the sweat-sheened torsos of laborers. I declined without hesitation, automatically, never having felt much rapport with Ginsberg from his writings, and because it wasn't within my range to give encouragement to a gay guy trying to pick me up, though it didn't bother me.

One job I never considered was table waiting. I couldn't have taken smiling at customers and being polite for tips all day.

If you could endure working somewhere for the statutory five months minimum, you'd try to handle it so that you were listed as having been let go for reasons beyond anyone's control, rather than fired for cause, because then you could collect unemployment checks.

There were ways of compensating for boring jobs: petty thievery of course, but my big illumination was the strategy of being so efficient and hardworking for the first three weeks that I'd look indispensable and could then slack for months before the first impression wore off. If I were lucky, I'd even have held on to enough respect that I could explain how personal problems had been undercutting my performance and the boss would lay me off and I could still cop the unemployment checks.

I'd been making an ignorant teenager's stabs at writing, without any real foundation of values except the most base, namely to express my poor, lonely, sentimental, grandiose, poetic self. I did have confidence in my insights into situations and people, and also in my basic aesthetic discrimination. But for the longest time (which at that age was three or four years) I was only a writer because I conceived of myself as one. I didn't write very much and what I wrote was not any good and it was mostly Dylan Thomas derived (one of my earliest New York poems began "Rain me green on stones unseething"). They were a lot about a desire to dissolve and about sex (coyly or under cover of symbols and similes) and about a fear of some horrible flaw in myself. As a poet or writer, I would become an example of how if you wear a mask long enough it becomes your face, or, to put it more kindly, how vocations often begin as poses.

I enrolled in a night poetry workshop at the New School in hopes of maybe meeting people who were interested in some of the same things as me. I had bad luck with that class, though I did meet a sad, hysterical girl with red capillaries on her nose and cheekbones, and large breasts that looked like twin Eeyores, who would let me have sex with her.

The guy who taught the class was a former poet named José Garcia Villa. "Former" because part of his self-dramatization was that in the late fifties he'd stopped writing in order "not to repeat" himself. He was Filipino, born in Manila in 1908, though he'd been in the U.S., mostly New York City, since he was twenty-one. He'd made a little literary splash in the forties and early fifties.

He was given to a poetic vocabulary not too far from Thomas's, maybe a tad more Blakean or Rilkean, if more limited, favoring words like "naked" and "bright" and "rose" and "lion"—but most especially and revealingly "I" and "God" (in both of whose ways he'd often instruct his readers)—in clean, aphoristic rows.

Anyway, he gave his classes in order to preside over a circle as much as anything else. Along with the proper class at the school on West Twelfth Street every week, there would be a social gathering at his apartment on Saturdays, and another one at a Smith's bar at Sixth Avenue and Fourteenth Street on Tuesdays. Everybody vied to be as debonairly supercilious, sexually insinuating, and sarcastic about poets of inferior sensibility as he was. I was the youngest student. Villa pronounced to all that I was "the most poetical looking" and one of the "sickest, which is a prerequisite for writing decent poems."

Whatever the direction I was going, I wanted to keep moving, and so, before 1967 was out, I'd started a poetry magazine with another student from the group named David Giannini. Giannini was about my age, had recently arrived in the city from New Jersey, and was poetry obsessed. He looked more Scandinavian than Italian—tall and muscular with thin blond hair, he wore wire-rimmed glasses, denim work shirts, corduroy jeans, and Hush Puppies. He worked out to stay buff and had a couple of slightly dumpy but definitely sexy longtime girlfriends we saw a lot of, who'd doted since high school on his po-eticalness and light sex japes. He liked to speak aphoristically too, like Villa, often making twinkling pronouncements, like "Picasso's nudes have blue periods," that were unequivocally insupportable.

True to our lyrical bent, we named the magazine *Genesis : Grasp*. The six issues we published across four years (1968–71) did present a beginning so early it's retardedly fetal. The first three issues were self-important, unfocused, and amateur, like a high school literary magazine. To give the magazine its due, it improved a lot by the final number, a double issue (#5/6). By then I'd moved a long way from my coeditor in tastes and attitude, and I edited the last three numbers (4 and 5/6) pretty much on my own. At that point I was printing them on a little $300 used tabletop offset printing press in my apartment, and typesetting the magazine on a rented IBM VariTyper.

I did have a little further public existence as a poet in those years. Once we started the magazine and I had written a file of poems, I sent a few to James Laughlin, publisher of New Directions Books, for him to consider for that year's New Directions *Annual*. To my mind, Laughlin's publishing company was the most prestigious in America. Not only was he Dylan Thomas's American publisher, but he also published Cé-line, Nabokov, Wilfred Owen, and Rimbaud (not to mention Henry Miller and William Carlos Williams and Ezra Pound), and many other of strictly the most literarily ambitious and adventurous international writers. The *Annual* was his hardcover anthology of new writing and had been coming out since the midthirties. In the 1970 edition he published eight poems of mine that I'd written in the previous couple of years, when I was eighteen and nineteen. They were awful—stilted and bombastic and sentimental. He published four more the following year and a couple of those were marginally better. But the better I got the less he seemed to like what I did. Still, I thought of New Directions as my publisher. Laughlin encouraged me to think he would eventually do a book of mine, but by the time I had put together one I liked, at age twenty-one or so, entitled *Baby Hermaphrodite Rabbits*, he didn't believe it would do. A few years later, once I'd been playing rock and roll for a while, I contacted him again, in hopes that he might be interested in commercial publication of a book for which I was responsible, with Tom, and in which I had complete confidence—*Wanna Go Out?* by Theresa Stern (about which, more later)—but he was scornful of it, and that was the end of our relationship.

CHAPTER SEVEN

A few days ago I went out for a walk by myself. My wife had been home sick for a while and we needed a break from each other. Two blocks from my apartment, along Eleventh Street between First and Second Avenues, I saw a pair of sneakers in the window of Tokyo Joe, a tiny Japanese-run consignment clothing store specializing in haute designers. I needed new sneakers and these looked great and never worn. They were low cut and form fitting in a complex web pattern of black and tomato-red leather sewn onto cream-colored suede, and made in Italy. They fit me perfectly and they only cost fifty-eight dollars, when they'd cost five times that new. I paid for them and said I'd pick them up in two or three hours, on my way back home.

It was a sunny, warm late afternoon in April. Further down the block, at the corner juice bar on Second Avenue, I got myself a take-out Full Meal Power blend of bananas, strawberries and apple juice with some kind of nutrition powder. It tasted like cold God.

I thought I'd stroll towards the West Village. A lot of people were out enjoying the weather. In Washington Square Park, the huge, rough, but delicately leaf-budding trees were pretty in a transvestite kind of way, but the park was mostly concrete and hard-packed dirt, and the large fountain pool in its central plaza was dry. The fountain had been appropriated, as it often is these years, by some dreary, fake-funny busker act whom a large touristy crowd on the fountain's perimeter was encouraging with self-congratulatory laughter and applause.

When I first left home and came to the city at seventeen, the park was glamorous for being where drugs were available to people who had no references. Vagrant kids with acoustic guitars hung out and hoped for action. It's the same now, only the heads are skate kids or stunt dancers instead of folksingers. Harmony Korine and his prep-school skate punks, including Chloë Sevigny, got their start in movies after being spotted there in the nineties.

I worked my way towards the street where my grandmother used to live. She died decades ago, but when I was a child, and then for my earliest years in New York, she lived at 72 Barrow Street. For me, the West Village—formerly plain Greenwich Village—will always be primarily the site of her apartment, and it's still my favorite neighborhood in Manhattan. Some of it is a tourist trap, but even the tourist attractions are relatively benign—"bohemian" cafés, chess clubs, music and guitar stores, sex-toy emporia, and leather-and-denim boutiques, rather than, say, the tacky Disney theater, franchise fast food, and rip-off "Must move! Going out of business!" electronics hawkers of the Times Square tourist trap uptown.

The core of the West Village is still a quiet tangle of narrow old tree-lined streets, some still cobblestoned. The tenements and brownstone apartment buildings, with their cast-iron stoop railings, and the small town houses, a few even made of wood, are some of the oldest in the city, and most are only three or four floors high, which makes the sky seem big. From the street, you can see through these homes' hefty double-hung windows how their rooms have high ceilings and wooden moldings and lots of bookshelves. On each block, a few of the ground floors host faded storefronts, like a little butcher shop or a laundromat, or bookstore, or pastry shop, or a tiny theater company or cabaret, or an eccentric restaurant. You know that many strangers have fallen in love with each other in those laundromats, especially when it was raining, whether they ever spoke or not.

My grandmother lived in one of four six-story buildings symmetrically enclosing a garden courtyard, on the northeast corner of Barrow and Hudson. The rough brick of the buildings is red-brown veined with sooty black, more like that of dismal row housing in industrial England than typical American brick, but it signified comfort to me.

Her apartment was tiny, smaller than the tenement apartment in which I've lived since 1975, which was already a few years after she'd died. She had a minuscule kitchen, a living room, a bathroom, and a bedroom, all small. The rooms were well lit by old casement windows with tarry putty squashed around their edges, and the floors were wood parquet, and there were prints on the walls and books on the shelves, plus the black and white Million Dollar Movie on TV. A dumbwaiter in the kitchen was used to lower trash to the basement on a certain schedule.

The few times we visited the apartment when I was a little kid, I couldn't sleep because I wasn't used to traffic noise, even from five stories above. I would lie in bed frustratedly sleepy, but also happy to be part of the huge activity of the city, the machinery of the night, a different night from Kentucky.

When I was a young teenager, the clothes in the shops on West Fourth Street were all eggplant and cream and tan colored, like "October in the railroad earth"—horizontal-striped T-shirts and thick dark-leather belts with big brass buckles, corduroy jeans, and boots, and work shirts, and suede and leather sports coats or work jackets. It's what the beatniks and folkies wore. On one visit I bought a Levi's suede cowboy jacket, same as their denim version, but suede. Even as a teenager, I still aspired a little to the cowboy.

Her apartment was like Superman's telephone booth to me; when I entered it I became another person, or the person I was to myself, rather than the person I was in everyday society. I became not only a citizen of Gotham but powerful and interesting, because she treated me like that.

During the first few months I lived in New York in 1967, she had me over to her apartment for dinner every week or two. After those first months I saw her less, and the last few times I saw her, a couple of years after I'd arrived, she was losing the ability to care for herself. I didn't have the maturity to know how to respond to that. I was spooked and bewildered. Her memory got bad, and the apartment became overrun by cockroaches, and she would fart continuously as she walked around, confused but chiding herself. Soon Aunt Phyllis and Uncle Dick took her in upstate, and a year or two later, when it got to where she needed constant attention, they put her in a nursing home.

Forty years later, I found myself gravitating towards her building as I walked from Washington Square a few blocks deeper west into the Village. Her street had hardly changed at all. It was quiet. The sidewalk entrance to her compound was set off by a high cast-iron archway under which a narrow shale path led between two of the buildings into her courtyard. The courtyard was eerily intimate, almost miniature— maybe fifty paces wide and another fifteen across. It was symmetrically divided into seven flower beds, their shapes formed by the crisscrossing stone walks linking the buildings' four doorways in the corners of the rectangular court. In the middle of the round center flower bed stood a wide, pitted stone urn on a pedestal. Beyond it, at the far edge of the enclosure, directly across from the path to the street, were two low spreading cherry trees. The ground ivy of each flower bed surrounded a broad stand of tulips blooming in four or five different monochromes. They were everywhere I looked. The flowers had that unconscious bounty that makes you understand how women get compared to flowers. Gratitude welled in me for the pure generosity of the flowers, not unlike the way I've been known to feel about a passing, unknown woman's breasts inside her sweater. I gazed at the cherry trees; they were in bloom, too. Their contorted, furrowed black branches were speckled and hidden by overlapping scribbles and billows of frothing pink that also made me want to thank someone. I tipped my head back. Way, way up high a balloon blew across the sky. Another one and then another one appeared, six or seven more in brilliant colors that rhymed with the tulips. I was conscious of my grandmother and her selfless love. I remembered how it was possible for such a thing to exist, and I felt grateful again, not just to have been the object of it, but to recall the way certain people are that pure, and then I felt my own pettiness fall away for a moment.

CHAPTER EIGHT

The first Central Park Human Be-In took place at the end of March 1967. "Be-In" makes me think "donut," internal donut. The DNA of humankind as stale crullers. I went up to the Sheep Meadow to take a look. People were standing around eyeing each other and some of them were wearing little bells on their clothes. There was face paint and flowers and pot smoking. Some kids were waving their arms and singing. The Sheep Meadow is big, and there were thousands and thousands there. Drugs were a theme, and people chanted about love. Most of them weren't really dressed right—just a hasty bead necklace or a hair daisy—but then neither was the Velvet Underground usually.

Like George Bush's flag waving after the World Trade Center attacks, the Be-In was more repellent for its assumption of an axiomatic underlying basis of unity than for the dubious underlying idea itself. For Bush's Americans that dubious idea was the virtue of self-righteous patriotism, and for the hippies it was the practicability of universal kindness and generosity. The people joined together by those unexamined assumptions seemed idiotic. On the other hand, my inability to fit in was involuntary too.

I was confused and disconcerted. Crowds bothered me, for one, and I knew I was badly flawed and I didn't see any way out of it. There was an exhilaration in the strength of the numbers though, and it did seem to promise that there would be serious consequences before the generation got old. It was spring in the ward.

I do remember once seeing a guy who was young and who had long blond hair and a handlebar mustache and a square jaw, back then. He was handsome and seemed self-confident and rich, looking around upstairs in the gallery of Gotham Book Mart with his friend. Maybe it was Dennis Hopper. He was probably someone like Dennis Hopper. Perhaps he helped organize the Woodstock festival. He was wearing a western suede jacket with very long fringe, including a row down the back of each sleeve, so his leather trailed psychedelically and swung, rippling, with casual cowboy majesty as he gestured. I envied him that jacket. I wished there was a world in which I could wear it. I'd dress Elizabethan style, myself, if I could get away with it.

At the beginning of June, two months after the Be-In, *Sgt. Pepper's Lonely Hearts Club Band* was released. I had to pretend to like it because it was played for me by this girl I'd met in the office where a temp agency had sent me that week. She had pot too. I wanted to fuck her so much. My facial expressions, speech, and gestures were the unprepossessing facade on a huge warehouse of hope to fuck. She was short and perky, with that little dash of a nose-tip and the disproportionately large nostrils that say "nose job." She had pretty skin—poreless, white, and smooth. I was a beardless seventeen-year-old stick figure, all wrists and ankles, with rumpled hair starting to cover my ears, archaic T. S. Elliot round tortoiseshell glasses, work shirt, jeans, and little status beyond dispossessed youth. I did look like a poet. I had deep-set eyes and thick lips and I smoked Lucky Strikes. Nan was probably five years older than me.

She lived in a renovated apartment on Second Avenue near Fifth Street, a single room filled with candles and batik pillows. I was depending on the implications of her willingness to smoke grass alone with me. The Beatles record had come out the day before. She played it on a portable stereo. I grew up on the Beatles. They were exciting when I was in the eighth grade. It was dewy, highly delineated, cute rock and roll. The new record was embarrassing. The band was presenting itself in a winking music-hall getup, with a lot of dramatic orchestration, to explain social problems to us. The public-event nature of the album's release, following from the Beatles' incredible popularity, was like the Academy Awards on TV, glitzy but dull, and left me feeling not so much let down as left out, elsewhere, and a little tacky by association.

I acted impressed for Nan's sake, as you would for a stranger telling you a personal anecdote, especially if she was wearing a very short skirt. I'm not saying I wasn't boring too. I was. Did that mean I'd have to do without sexual intercourse? No!

We rolled a joint, lit some candles, and turned off the lamps. I succeeded with Nan but it was hard work, and, as usual, still hard work once I'd gotten my dick inside her. As the sex act proceeded, she behaved like she was resisting it. She didn't fight, just passively refused to participate. But I was no epicurean voluptuary myself. I probably wasn't even putting my mouth between a girl's legs yet, at least not with any skill (though the fact is a girl like Nan, back then, would probably have been so embarrassed by it that it would have turned her off and she'd have discouraged me).

In those days girls didn't groom their pubic hair. That was sexy—it was an animalistic sign of individuality, despite a girl's otherwise carefully managed appearance. Nan's pussy got damp but not soaking wet. It was slick, like a squeaky rubber duck. Of course I ejaculated within seconds of squeezing my hard-on into it. Then it was back to having to try to think of something to talk about and trying to seem relaxed, while the brain wheels spun like a car's in the mud.

By late 1967 I had an apartment on Sixth Street east of Second Avenue. It was one dark room and I was lonely there a lot. The loneliness was unpleasant but I came to think it was inevitable, not only because it never went away, but because there was a whole literature of alienation to go with it. There's a whole literature for every stage of maturity, but especially the earlier ones.

I worked at Gotham Book Mart in midtown for a while at this time. I learned a lot there. It was the most famous and the best literary bookstore in New York, probably in the whole world, in terms of inventory, and perhaps second only to Paris's Shakespeare & Company for literary associations. It had a huge out-of-print stock. Every year, for decades, the management had been saving and storing each year's unsold obscure and ambitious new poetry and fiction, as well as film literature, and all other high culture in printed form, much of it from esoteric small presses. The whole three-story building on Forty-Seventh Street was store property. Among the district's diamond merchants' shingles poked out the bookstore's little painted cast-iron sign of three fishermen in a rowboat, their pole lines down in the ripples, a catch bending each one's rod, above the caption "wise men fish here." Miss Steloff, the owner, who'd started the shop in 1920, was still there nearly every day.

The store had low ceilings and was a jumble. The floor-to-ceiling shelves that lined the walls, and the waist-high aisles of shelves and display tables in the rooms, were all home-carpentered in worn wood that was painted deep blue. Books and papers and pamphlets were stacked and stuffed on every surface. The wall shelves were "double packed"—meaning there was a row of books behind the visible ones. Mr. Lyman, the harried store manager, who always wore a white dress shirt, tie, and pressed slacks, was a thin, stiffly upright, cartoonishly bland-featured man who wore black-rimmed glasses on a tense face that reddened under the nonstop pressure. He was like a character from a Victorian novel—it seemed as if the store was his whole world. Or like he was a military lifer, getting all his pride and dignity from his commitment to the service, like a mildly femme and nervous James Stewart in the Victor McLaglen role in a John Ford cavalry movie. It was a serious enterprise up there, and they all regarded themselves as devoted servants of the writers and their literate public.

I arrived at the same time as Andy Brown, who'd been chosen from among applicants by the aged Miss Steloff to buy the store from her. One of his first projects was an inventory, and I got assigned to help catalog the hundreds and hundreds of old literary magazines, many in complete runs, that filled a storage room on the second floor. I spent day after day alone up there, crouched at the bottom of the shelves, turning over in my hands such signifying artifacts as T. S. Eliot's august *Criterion* ("it must be said"); Harriet Monroe's *Poetry* when it was publishing Pound's circle in the teens and twenties (Pegasus Chicago); Eugene and Maria Jolas's Paris journal *Transition*, where a lot of early modernists and surrealists appeared (champagne, frottage); Princess Caetani's *Botteghe Oscure* (Renaissance print shop), a gorgeous high-toned bohemian thing from Rome; Wyndham Lewis's British magazine *Blast* (Lewis with his hair on fire); Margaret Anderson's *The Little Review* (grid of tweedy breasts); Charles Henri Ford's *View*, where all the 1940s temporarily New York European Dadaists/surrealists like Breton and Man Ray and Max Ernst published (avid narcissism of bohemian style); Ashbery's and Koch's and Schuyler's and Mathews's *Locus Solus* (swoon of witty word chess); Diane Di Prima's and LeRoi Jones's *The Floating Bear* (a bear who can't drown because he's a doodle) . . . The array seemed to embody the separate camps of all the assertive sensibilities of the century in bound-paper containers of their representation. (My very favorite literary magazine, though I didn't discover it till a few years later—the greatest literary magazine of the twentieth century—was a clumsy, cheap, legal-sized, stapled mimeo, published on the Lower East Side, 1963–1966, called simply *C*, edited by Ted Berrigan. You could extrapolate everything worthwhile in the universe from its thirteen issues, and you'd have a great time, giggling.)

At the Gotham I met a guy who recommended that my *Genesis : Grasp* coeditor and I move to Santa Fe, New Mexico, where it'd be cheaper to live and get printing done, as well as being pretty and quiet. We were curious about the desert, as well as kind of nervous about how we were going to be able to afford to publish the magazine in New York, so we decided to try it, and signed up for a driveaway car, which I totaled in Illinois, drunk. (I called its owner in Texas to inform him. He didn't yell at me but just chillingly whispered, "Oh no.") We took a bus the rest of the way.

Living in Santa Fe was like a prolonged case of that feeling you get when you wake up in the morning and don't really want to get out of bed yet and face the day, but then can only doze a little—which is actually more exhausting than being awake is—unable to fall fully back asleep, and you stretch out the postponement of getting out of bed way too long, into brainlessness like the inside of your head has turned to chalk.

The town was a backwater, and worse was the mediocre-artist demographic, with its pretense that it had rejected corrupt worldly striving for natural Santa Fe. There was no one to talk to. We got a spacious but unheated flattop adobe house, set on a slope on the edge of town, for $50 a month. A violent alcoholic Chicano Vietnam vet lived in a house down the hill, and he'd come up to drink and rant every day or two. I liked him but in small doses. The center of town was a long, dull walk away for groceries.

Our finest moment there was getting a poem from Allen Ginsberg for the magazine, which he'd kindly sent on receipt of our pathetic solicitation, and then rejecting it. It didn't meet our standards of craftsmanship. He wrote a cold angry couple of sentences back. We literally did not know what we were doing.

I did find a pretty girlfriend, kind of the low-energy teenage Marlon Brando girl of Santa Fe. She was inarticulate but broody and rebellious and dressed in a black turtleneck and jeans. Her parents worked at the tiny local college, St. John's. As usual, though, sex was tense and claustrophobic, like it was a room that had those infrared alarm beams crisscrossing it, like in jewel-heist movies. Everything seemed to set off uncertainty and remorse. And the social part before and after was no more relaxed than that either. (This is all in hindsight. Like the loneliness, the difficult sex seemed normal at the time. God knows I craved it.)

We'd been in Santa Fe for two months or so when Giannini's draft board contacted him and he had to return to New Jersey. That was enough to decide us the experiment was over. He flew home, and soon after I hitchhiked back to New York. In those days hitchhiking was still common. It was illegal on the big interstates but there were plenty of other well-traveled roads to thumb, and it was easy enough to station yourself at the entrance ramps to the interstates, too. In the Midwest somewhere, on my way back to New York, a farmer brought me home to his family's big noisy dinner table piled with steaming fresh vegetables and butter and bread and iced tea and ham and fried chicken, like out of a cowboy movie, and I slept for a night on their living room couch.

A couple of days later I got drenched in a sustained rainstorm at dusk on a shelterless two-lane where no car stopped.

I got back to New York City fine, though, and that was the only time I've ever tried to live anywhere else.

CHAPTER NINE

n 1968 I held a series of jobs, most rewardingly at the Strand Book Store among a crew of other artistically inclined kids. I worked in the basement packing books for shipping. But the year slipped past in a static-y, routine montage of menial employment, awkward romantic relationships, forced tortured writing, and unskilled magazine editing.

With girlfriend Marianne, 1968

One notable event was that I received my orders to appear in the fall before the Selective Service. I was eighteen and eligible for the draft. The Vietnam War was raging.

There were lots of stories about how a guy could get away with presenting himself as homosexual or crazy or drug addicted to get out of the draft. I couldn't see doing that. It would grate too much on my self-respect to let the government turn me into an elaborate liar. It wasn't really a principle, just a natural reaction. I realize that the attitude was a luxury. My ambivalence about faking would probably keep me from being able to pull it off anyway. I wasn't going to claim to be a conscientious objector either. I could imagine wars I'd fight, and I didn't want to go into alternative service.

I finally decided to go to the induction center and do whatever came naturally, to just trust my honest responses. The army could not really want someone like me.

The day came and I stood in line with the other candidates in an ugly institutional examination room. The physical was routine and inoffensive, and then we were led to a classroom where we were given papers with multiple-choice questions on them. My indignation started to build. The questions were stupid and boring and obnoxious, and I didn't feel like submitting. I stood up and left the room. There must have been an official present, but I don't remember. It wasn't a situation where they'd physically prevent someone from leaving.

The halls of the building were dead quiet; everyone was behind closed doors. I wandered around uncertainly for a minute or two before an officer walked by and asked what I was doing in the hallway. I told him I'd been taking the written test but had gotten fed up with it. He asked me if I wanted to see a psychiatrist and I said OK. He took me to an office.

In the office was a shrink straight from Central Casting. He not only had a goatee but he had a Viennese accent. He asked me vut zeh pkroblem was and I told him I resented the written test, that the questions were insulting and that's why I'd stopped answering them. I told him I didn't think there'd be any point in putting me in the army. I was a high school dropout who couldn't hold a job and a lot of the reason was that I was a loner who'd never been part of any organization and I couldn't stand authority. I knew what would happen if I was drafted into the army—I'd end up in the brig. What would be the point of that? I meant what I said, and I guess I was convincing because I was given a psychological deferral.

Tom and I wrote each other letters sporadically. He had ended up graduating from public high school in Wilmington and then enrolled in a university in the Carolinas somewhere, but he quickly dropped out. By the end of the year he moved up to the East Village.

Right away we began spending most of our spare time together. Our mentalities got intermixed. When we didn't have girlfriends, we'd be together for days on end except when we were at work. We shared apartments for short periods, but even when we had our own places, half the time one of us would find himself at the other's so late at night that the visitor would just crash on the floor, and we'd keep talking across the rooms in a lazy artillery of cartoon characters, César Vallejo, and guck-sicles that would continue as we read our books, maybe him up in his loft bed, me with a blanket and pillow on the floor in the next room, for another hour before we passed out. People thought we were brothers. We were the same height and had the same skinny, wide-shouldered builds. Our speech tones and patterns even became similar—people mistook us for each other on the phone.

Those years—1969 to 1974, from when Tom got to New York until we began playing at CBGB with our band Television—seem to have lasted such a long time, to have contained more than could be possible, because everything was new and made such strong impressions on us and we were changing so quickly. But during the time itself, those four or five years felt like forever for the opposite reason: that there was nothing to do. But our ennui actually contributed to our sense of freedom—we were so bored and isolated we might try anything.

For a few months in the spring of 1969, we shared an apartment on Eleventh Street just west of Second Avenue. It was a typical little three-room shotgun flat five or six floors up in a tenement. The refrigerator had been leaking on the kitchen floor and the landlord had ignored our complaints. One boring afternoon we squeezed it through the window to the airshaft. There's not a much better-feeling suspense than that endless second or two during which a heavy machine is falling from a great height.

Now and then, when we were walking down a street together, we'd hunch forward and begin to buzz with our mouths and flap our elbows, and do figure eights along the curb and gutter for a block or two, fertilizing the parking meters.

Every few weeks the two of us would have enough money between us to go have a drink at a bar. We shared pretty much everything we had, except girlfriends. Since neither of us had anything, it evened out. We'd spring for expensive bar booze, rather than an occasional quart of beer at home, to check out artists' bars, where we thought we might find good-looking girls who had the right values. Max's Kansas City was the paradigm. Other bars would ascend to be briefly as hip as Max's and then sink again. A new artists' bar that year was St. Adrian's, at the Broadway Central Hotel on Broadway at Third Street. The hotel was a huge old flophouse that extended all the way back to the next street over, Mercer. (Three years later it would host, in its backside there, the Mercer Arts Center, where the New York Dolls were the house band at the Oscar Wilde Room.) St. Adrian's occupied the hotel's entire ground floor, with a very long bar. Sleek, long-legged girls who had clean hair and fresh clothes crowded the space. Some people had paint spatters on their pants, some wore sunglasses.

One night at St. Adrian's we hit pay dirt. Two girls talked to us and bought us drinks and invited us to their table. They were older than we were and less inhibited than us and obviously had more money. Everybody got drunk. Eventually one of them, Patty, came back to our apartment with Tom and me. Tom and I shared a big double mattress on the floor. There wasn't any other furniture in the apartment except some milk-crate shelving and some cushions and a couple of kitchen chairs at a kitchen table. The three of us, too drunk to do anything else, lay down in bed. It was dark. I didn't know what Tom was thinking, but I was not going to let this chance to have sex with Patty go by. I took the initiative and she and I started kissing. Tom went up on the roof to sleep. She gave me her phone number when she left the next morning. I called a week or two later, and we ended up in a romance that interrupted for almost two years the life I'd been leading with Tom.

It turned out that she was the wife of Claes Oldenburg, the pop artist famous for his sculptures, soft and otherwise, giant and otherwise, of food and appliances and generic household doodads. When I met her, Patty and Claes were getting divorced after nine years together, during which she had been his muse and expeditor. She was seamstress of his sculptures and frequent star of his Happenings. He had recently moved out of their fifth-floor loft, just east of First Avenue on Fourteenth Street.

The loft was spectacular, stretching an entire block in length, from Fourteenth Street back to another entrance on Thirteenth Street, and the whole width of an old factory building, about as wide as a tenement building. I'd never seen anything like it. The living space, half a block deep (about forty-five yards) on the Fourteenth Street end, was separated into four white-painted rooms lit by big windows (the building was taller than adjacent buildings, so the loft had windows going along the sides of it, as well as onto Fourteenth Street and Thirteenth Street). The industrial entrance door from the fifth-floor landing led into the dining room, which was empty except for a rope hammock and a little glass cabinet of some drippily painted life-size plaster cakes and hamburgers of Claes's. The main room, beyond the dining room, fronted onto Fourteenth Street and was more than twice the size of the dining room. A double bed was parked along the wall, but that area was also the living room, with a couch and some chairs and a glass coffee table. Against the wall past the bed were bookshelves of art books and New York poetry. Down in the far reaches towards Fourteenth Street was a life-sized biplane framework, a giant hardwood replica of the balsa skeleton of a model plane, hung with Christmas tree lights.

The kitchen, with its long shiny wooden table, was on the other side of the dining room. The portable record player was usually in the kitchen too, because that's where we sat around. There was always a fifth of Johnnie Walker Red, my arbitrary drink of choice, in reach there, provided by Patty. Past the kitchen was a smaller room with another bed. That second-bedroom section of the loft was divided lengthwise to include, alongside the bedroom, a very large bathroom that had a gigantic tub in the middle of it.

There was recent New York art on all the walls—Andy Warhol silkscreen paintings, plenty of Claes, Lucas Samaras, Öyvind Fahlström, Jim Dine.

This was half the loft, the Fourteenth Street side. The Thirteenth Street end had been Claes's studio. It was cavernous, without dividing walls and unrenovated. The bare brick perimeter was dark and dusty, the ceilings splintery rafters and planks, and the floors were the worn unfinished wood of an old-fashioned city factory. Windows lined the long brick side walls. A lot of Claes's collection of little dime-store knickknacks and generic clothing and pieces of hardware and magazine ads and small shiny toys, etc., that would become his hallucinatorily magical Mouse Museum was scattered around on shelves and tabletops, and there were unfinished sculptures and ragged pieces of fragile early works of sloppily painted papier-mâché supermarket-ware logos, or dust-thick big canvas sculptures of diner food here and there, down the room. It was fantastic.

I didn't take all this in immediately. It took weeks to learn about what was what in the apartment, who was who around Patty and what they'd done, what her life had been in the previous few years. At the beginning, she was just a funny rich chick who liked my company and took good care of me and loved having sex. We were always laughing. And though, yes, she had all the money she needed, she was no kind of snob. She was really a working-class Polish kid from Milwaukee, with no sense of economic entitlement. She was like the wiseass, hardass chicks I went to junior high school with in Lexington, only she was an artist and she'd been in the middle of things in American art for the past few years. She hadn't actually been making art herself for quite a while, but she'd come to New York to do that at the end of the fifties, when she was just out of art school, and she was now as sophisticated about art and the "art scene" as anybody else in that world. She knew that half the people in it were crooks and that, when not creepy, the art world was largely a circus and a game, but that a lot of the players in it were amusing, interesting people, and she respected the making of real art probably more than any other human undertaking. She took

At the beginning, she was just a funny rich chick who liked
my company and took good care of me and loved having sex.

it all lightly—and pleasure and wit were what mattered—but she was soulful too.

A tense night towards the end of our relationship was partly salvaged when she remarked wistfully, "Absolutes make the heart go flounder." How could you not love someone who could say something like that? Another thing she said once was, "A fool and her money are soon po-eted." Also, "Unhappiness is just another form of happiness."

She was a firecracker, small and bow-legged and quick, with a pretty little hard ass. She had stringy, greasy peroxide-blond hair and a wide flat Slavic face that was also a bit hard. She strutted like a sexy girl-rooster, often in a teeny brown leather miniskirt or a short, silky, leopard-print wrap dress.

It was impressive to be with her in high-pressure situations, like, say, when she had to deal with the emotional repercussions of some contact with Claes, such as when we went to his big opening at the Museum of Modern Art. I could see that she felt a little shaken, challenged, being the ex-wife, and one who'd played such a big role in the creation of the art, but it stimulated her and she would come through, wisecracking, in a way that didn't leave room for doubt, disarming any potential intimidators. She was like a tough Howard Hawks broad, the life of the party, who would fall in love with an impossible person but always bob to the top no matter how rough it might get.

The program was that I'd come over to her place after work (when I was working—for weeks at a time she'd more or less take care of me) and we'd sit in the kitchen smoking grass, drinking scotch, with a record playing—Aretha Franklin, or Bob Dylan, say ("Respect" and "Call Me" and "Belle Isle")—and she'd make us a salad and baked potato and broil a couple of very good thick steaks. Then we'd keep drinking the scotch, and smoking, until we went to bed and watched a little Johnny Carson and Joe Franklin maybe, and then have sex two or three times. I've read that a man's sex drive peaks at nineteen, while a woman's does at thirty-five. She was thirty-four and nine or ten months when we met and I was nineteen.

Larry Rivers, the hawk-nosed, fast-talking painter who was a bridge between abstract expressionism and pop and who was close to Frank O'Hara and all the other first-generation New York poets, lived in the loft above Patty's. (Patty's best friend was Larry's British wife—from whom he'd been separated for a while—Clarice, formerly nanny for his kids. Clarice, who was in her early thirties too, was a funny party person herself, one of whose conspirators in those days was Jim Carroll, who was my age. One time Patty was on the phone when I arrived and when she hung up she told me she'd been speaking to Clarice, who was in her Central Park West bedroom putting women's makeup on Jim. That sounded really glamorous and I was a little jealous.) Larry could hear the sound of us having sex coming from Patty's loft underneath his the same as we could hear him honking on his sax at four AM. A couple of years later I learned that he'd drilled a peephole into his floor directly above Patty's bed to supplement our noises. Patty told me he sometimes called me "Tarzan."

Our time together was dramatic. She was headstrong, while I had a lot of pride even though I was a self-conscious innocent in her world. I actually hit her in the face one time—the only time I've ever hit a girl who didn't want me to. We were on a road trip in the South and I was driving and she wouldn't stop harassing me and I pulled off the road and smacked her. But I was often consternated in gatherings of her friends. They were all twenty years older than me and successful and famous and had known each other forever. If the group was smaller, it could be a lot more comfortable. The best artists were the kindest. I loved Rauschenberg. He was so generous and considerate. I had a great couple of lunches with Patty and Jasper Johns too. He was mandarin, but always wittily, nicely, teasingly. Probably my fondest memory of an encounter like that was the day Patty and Clarice and I spent with de Kooning at the house and studio he'd designed for himself in East Hampton, and then driving around with him and walking along the Atlantic. I was ignorant though. Something came up that afternoon that drew a Lautréamont reference from me and I was privately astounded that de Kooning responded with more Lautréamont. I didn't think painters knew anything about writing.

Eventually, after a year and a half together, it was time for Patty and me to separate. Technically it was my decision, but it was obvious to us both that the gap in our ages and social circles was decisive finally; it was wisest to preempt, as much as we loved each other (we're still friends). The finish came when she offered to take me with her on a trip of a month or two to Europe. I didn't want to live off of her on that scale, but she might well go alone if I didn't come, and I knew she'd have wild adventures there and that it would be the equivalent of our separating. I could see it was time to detach. It was emotional.

In the midst of the weeks of splitting up I turned twenty-one—she was thirty-seven then—and she made me a birthday dinner. It started with LSD, and then a feast of my favorite foods. She gave me a ten-speed racing bike too (I would sell it almost immediately). At a certain point she innocently remarked, "You're only twenty-one once, you know," and it caught me by surprise. I'd never quite understood time that way. I could never have a twenty-first birthday again. I started crying and then so did she and we were both sobbing.

From the notebooks and diaries I kept at that time I can see that I haven't really changed much since then. I've learned things, about writing and other means of expression for instance, and learned other behaviors, but it's that development of skills and further branching of behaviors that is the difference, not me myself, not what underlies the outer appearances. Of course what's deepest down inside is boring; it's actually the surface that's interesting, even though it's often deceptive. We're probably all the same as each other deep down inside. (As Ron Padgett put it, "Am I a good person? Yes, after / a certain point, and no, after another. / Deep down I'm just down there, a kind of gurgling / black Jell-O that doesn't have any idea / of what's going on up here[. . .]") A little above that, but still underneath the outward signs of a person, are the emphases that define one's practical range of character, the realistic limitations to one's identity. But we're usually assessed according to our social existence. That's not really any more fair than being judged by how well we make art.

Still, it's what's interesting, whether that's "fair" or not. People don't really have the right to take credit for themselves at all. Ultimately, not only are we all the same, but what happens is out of our control. I suppose that's what religions are about—coming to terms with the way that behind the veil, nobody is different from anyone else, much less better, and no one even has any real control over phenomena, including themselves—and is the sense in which religions are true, recommending, under the circumstances, surrender to "God" (which is to say, acceptance of "what happens"). All there is are the entertainments, pastimes, of love and work, the hope of keeping interested.

CHAPTER TEN

moved directly from Patty's to a place I'd gotten with a girl I'd recently met. Her name was Anni and she was just out of a midwestern university art program, working as an assistant to the sculptor Marisol. She was pale and tall and skinny with tightly curly, Orphan Annie–style big red hair and freckles. Her smile looked like a nervous, questioning, determined-to-please child's, like her face was being stretched back from her ears, her inner eyebrows pointing upward, as if there should have been little sweat droplets flying from her forehead. It rent my heart. She had a willfully cheerful personality that mixed whimsy with wide-eyed morbidity.

Anni worked hard making artworks out of unusual materials, like tiny plastic doll accessories and flexible transparent plastic sheeting that she would sew things into, an iconography of rag dolls and Marilyn. She drew a lot with colored pencils. She was a good draftsman. The artworks were also cheerful in a childlike way, but so extremely as to seem possibly hostile and threatening. I worried about how the world would treat her.

We'd found a small room-and-a-fraction in a cheap factory building erected in the mid-nineteenth century as an armory. It was on Mott Street in Little Italy, diagonally opposite the primitive, rose-beige "old St. Patrick's"—a two-hundred-year-old church (not the famous, more recent, uptown cathedral). Harvey Keitel prayed there in Scorsese's early movies. We were the only tenants who actually lived in our building—technically illegally. The five-story warren of repair shops and small manufacturers went dead silent and spooky at night. Its shadowy rooms and passages were dirty, damp, gray-painted brick and plaster. The building extended deep belowground too, in multiple low-ceilinged sub-basements that looked as if illicit medical procedures or interrogations took place there.

I was doing psychedelic drugs every few weeks: mushrooms and THC and acid. We had a friend named James who was a student at Yale who tripped with us sometimes. He was short, with a Beatles-style bowl cut—a friendly, fast-talking, analytical guy full of observations and theories who was attracted to the bohemian otherworldliness of our household. That period will forever be signified for me by the most psychedelic piece of writing I know of: the words that appeared, purplish-black and burnt-looking, the way drilled teeth smell, when James and Anni and I in turn, stoned on mushrooms, struck typewriter keys that smacked their heads through the ink ribbon into a fibrous sheet of typing paper, each in our attempt to spell the word "psilocybin," thereby inadvertently producing, in the form of the type-indented sheet, a 2-and-a-half-D trigger for mushroom flashbacks.

Another time, I OD'd on THC. Sometimes a powdered concentrate of it would come to market and it was strong. I snorted it. On that night I was alone in the apartment, if "apartment" is the word. It was a brutally plain cubicle with a sink, as well as one tiny corner enclosure where we put a bed. We had a little refrigerator and a hot plate. The toilets were generic institutional multistalls in the hall. Our loft was more like a bomb shelter than an apartment, but I wasn't consciously aware of how grim it was. I was just playing house there. It wasn't an ideal environment for a psychedelic overdose, though, especially a solitary one.

I lay in the small bed in a fetal position with my eyes closed. Any sensory input was too much, though the places where my mind went, when closed off in itself, were also scary. Everything was so tense that the bottomless quiet of late night in the empty building was like a carnival haunted house—I'd be startled by some barely audible creak or snap, which it would then take three endless seconds for my consciousness to classify as nonthreatening and my pulse twenty seconds to recover from. For hours I lay in bed trying to remain still and limp. I'd keep my eyes closed until that would start to panic me too, and then I'd open them long enough to make sure I wasn't somewhere scarier than my room, and then because that was too bright and cold and dirty I'd close them again. I dispersed evenly. At my most solid I was a set of molecules coalesced in an illusion of more or less cooperative operation, but the true nature and function of which was to ricochet and zoom around randomly in the void. I was permeable and undefined, space itself, meaningless cause and effect, like the rest of the universe, rather than a being of volition. Life was an extended car wreck. I tried to be patient enough as I waited for the drugs to wear off that I didn't make things worse.

Finally, also, at this time, despite my natural alienation from society, I was becoming affected by the American political situation. Things had become so extreme that you were confronted everywhere, every day, with the conflicts. Nobody trusted or respected anybody. Nearly everybody thought they had the answers but nobody agreed with anybody else. Frightened and distraught and angry writings about Vietnam and Nixon fill my notebooks from the time. I especially sympathized with the Black Panthers and hated and despised Nixon and was horrified by what was happening in Vietnam, but all I ever did was express those feelings in journals and in talks with friends. I didn't vote or march or write letters or contribute money. I had no conception of an effective resistance. I didn't feel effectual, but like a particle that was being slapped around among all the others. The adult, administered world was comprehensible psychologically, but it operated in another dimension, was something that took place on the other side of the screen. I didn't feel much different towards it than I had to the school authorities or to parents when I was a kid. They were oppressive but eternal, just something to escape.

When I left Anni, after a few months, I moved to an apartment two blocks away, at 173 Elizabeth Street, just past the southwest corner of Elizabeth and Spring, in the heart of Little Italy. I was working on what would be the final and best issue of *Genesis : Grasp*, a double issue, number 5/6. I'd bought a cheap used offset printing press from a repair shop in the Mott Street building and was doing the printing myself. Tom and I resumed our old inseparability, which would last for most of the coming three or four years.

The Elizabeth Street apartment was great, the best I'd ever had. It took up the whole top floor of a rickety tenement owned by the two old Italian brothers who ran the little grocery store in the building next door. It had four small rooms, arranged in a U shape, with the building's stairwell, on the other side of my walls, in the middle of the U. The front door opened into the kitchen, and the kitchen led through an archway—there were no doors inside the apartment—into another little room where I put the printing press (which was only the size of a milk crate), which led to the right into the room containing my narrow bed, which, in another right turn, opened into the living room,

In the Mott Street loft, 1971.

which had a little sealed-up fireplace. Both the living room and kitchen had windows onto Elizabeth Street. The other two rooms each had a little, high, square window with an inward-opening wooden cover, like something in an old monastery, facing out back across the roofs. The floors slanted because the building was so old and settled and warped. The plaster on the walls was as fissured and dimensional and glowy as the encaustic of a Johns painting. In the mornings I would hear a rooster crowing. Sometimes I'd see him, white but tinged with soot, a naked red crest on his head and a drooping, flopping version of that under his beak, strutting around on the rooftop across the street.

Tom was amused by the one tiny, thin, dented and burnt wire-handled pot I had, which I used to make oatmeal or boil water for instant coffee. (I don't think I ever bought any pots and pans until I was over thirty-five—there'd always be enough junk for my purposes lying in a cabinet or drawer in every new place.) That pot was so ancient and damaged, it transported Tom to the battle of Antietam. Another thing that made an impression on him was the old label-free peanut butter jar in which I kept a dead turtle, as a sort of decoration or artwork, leaking its fluids.

Tom was working in a storefront bakery in the West Village, which was run by an Eastern spiritual sect. He had a solo late-night shift bagging bread. I hung with him there some nights. The loaves were very dense and heavy and supposedly nutritious. We got an unlimited supply for ourselves, and often the only food in my apartment would be a round brick or two of the bread, mayonnaise, and instant coffee. I subsisted for days on nothing else, except maybe a slice or two of pizza.

Tom and I bought books when we had any pocket change and then sold some of them when we were desperate. Back then, both sides of Fourth Avenue from Ninth Street to Fourteenth Street were lined almost entirely with used-book stores. Books were just about our only liquid assets. We would never sell the guitar or typewriter, and they were so beat up they had no pawn value.

By this time, every other job Tom and I got was in a used-book store, and rummaging through them was our main form of recreation as well—just to get out in the air and dig around. I had accounts at both Gotham and the Phoenix Book Shop on Jones Street in the West Village. The Phoenix was a hole in the wall run by an impatient, prissy guy named Bob Wilson. Wilson cared about poor poets and their poetry, though, and he'd give you respect if you had knowledge. The poetry section at the Phoenix always yielded a softly glowing little pamphlet or two that worked on our feelings and pleasure centers.

Then there was the little bookshop on Perry Street in the West Village, which Tom and I loved especially, because its proprietor, Mr. Sackin, made us so happy. I think the shop was called Perry Street Books. Mr. Sackin was an old man, like a quiet preoccupied balding small chicken or albino mole, whom we imagined as being perfectly gentle and humble and innocent. He was completely oblivious to us.*

Tom and Anni would come over and help me with printing and collating as I worked on putting together the new issue of the magazine. I had a couple of other friends I published in it too. One I met through Joel Fisher, who was a sculptor interested in paper. We included a work by Joel stapled into each copy of *Genesis : Grasp* number 4, a blank scrap of rough paper that, though it wasn't relevant to disclose in the issue, was made of pulp created in Joel's digestive system. He'd eaten nothing but

---

* We wrote our first collaborative poem in his honor, "Ode to Mr. Sackin." It contained lines like:

> I fanned myself with Mary Magdalene. Now that she is you
> I still don't believe me.
> Like a dot in the shark
> my closets flower into decadent empires
> where there are no bookworms.
> I am a hack and you, Mr. Sackin, are the hackee

and

> It was a rotten idea.
> My festering dragon
> nudges against your trousers. He wants something
> good to read.
> We know you'll have the book Mr. Sackin because you're a fuckhead.

It was more or less the way we talked to each other, and, in its written form, it was the beginning of a pastime, a recreation, that eventually resulted in our book, *Wanna Go Out?* by Theresa Stern.

paper for a few days and then made fresh sheets from what came out of his butt. This person Joel introduced me to, Steven Schomberg, hung out at a chess club in the West Village. He was a little older than me, dark complected, plump, and hairy. His hair, black, was not long but profuse, hard to keep shaved on his face, and it curled from the edges of his dirty dime-store clothes. He sweated a lot. He was cheerful and driven. He'd fill a couple of thick notebooks every month. They were magnificent. He didn't distinguish mass media from actual social interactions. In the notebooks he made small talk with women who flaunted their erogenous zones in porn magazines, and he got advice from comics superheroes. He pasted clipped imagery from porn and comics into the composition books, above handwritten captions, along with his colorful drawings, sometimes painted in hobby-model enamel, and his diagrams of scientific ideas and of visitors from outer space, as well as cursive prophetic stories about science and philosophy and celebrities and memories and predictions and personal knowledge and insights. By the time he finished with one of the half-inch-deep books with its black-and-white marbled covers, it would be swollen to three inches thick. I published some excerpts from one of them in that final issue of *Genesis : Grasp*.

Another guy I had a lot of contact with that year was Simon Schuchat. Simon was a sixteen-year-old who'd sent some poems to the magazine. I liked his writing a lot and eventually extracted a pamphlet from him that we published as one of the two "subscriber supplements" to *Genesis : Grasp* number 5/6. (Beginning with issue number 4, issues came with a young writer's first book—5/6, being a double issue, came with Ernie Stomach's *uh* as well as Simon's *Svelte*. Ernie Stomach was really me—at the time I had the vague intention of spending the rest of my life writing under four or five completely separate distinct identities.) Simon went to high school in Washington, DC. He loved the New

York poets, the St. Mark's poets—New York School poets, first and second generations—whatever you want to call them. Schuchat would get up to New York whenever he could and he'd split his time between hanging with me and dropping in on Anne Waldman and Michael Brownstein and Ted Berrigan. He was a hefty guy with long hair who spoke in a ceaseless monologue. He just poured out talk, not frantically, but in a steady stream, rarely smiling, his face sweating a little. He liked a cigar. He was droll and romantic and resigned.*

I was ready to move on though. The magazine had run its course. I thought I'd start a new publishing venture called *The Philosophical Review* to fulfill the promise of identity-sabotaging invention, mockery, despair, and musicality that we had begun to approach in the final issue or two of *Genesis : Grasp*. But within a year and a half, music would come to dominate.

---

* An untitled poem of Simon's from *Genesis : Grasp* number 5/6:

> when it is too late to turn on the TV
> and the cold whisper seeps into your hands
> as the night gets progressively wet
> stop for a second to smile at cowboys
> who clatter over stones to ranchlands
> where immense lines of indians
> walk along cold night speed rivers
> as grey wind slams shatters windows
> and old heads stare drunk in the glass

CHAPTER ELEVEN

By 1971 Tom had found the apartment on Eleventh Street where he'd live for the next few years—322 East Eleventh, between First and Second Avenues. It was a small three-room railroad apartment on the second floor, in back. As usual, the front door opened into the kitchen, where the bathtub was too, and, facing into the kitchen from that doorway, the living room was to the left, with windows out into sunlit paved yards and alleys, and a tiny dark bedroom to the right, its bed a platform up near the ceiling to preserve floor space underneath. The little water-closet toilet was beyond the bedroom.

That apartment of his takes up a big area in my memories. It was in the center of our territory in the East Village. I spent half my time at his place. It's where we would write *Wanna Go Out?* as well as write and rehearse and cassette-record our first songs.

My apartment on the top floor on Elizabeth Street, in contrast, reverberated like a gothic bell with loneliness and frustration. I would lie on the bed there and stare at the wall, shaken, oppressed, the jar of dead turtle ensconced on its desk shelf in the next room, the flat's slanted floors cold expressionism, a tiny poetry press in the passage behind me, the empty refrigerator beyond that. I felt like a vampire there, someone with secrets from everyone, who, by that token, was cheating and exploiting everyone, especially the girls I used for sex and ego caresses, without usually finding very much more to be interested in about them, well aware that this was my own failing.

At Tom's there was strength in numbers, even if the numbers were only one, two. There were lots of things we could say to each other and ways we could behave that no one else we knew appreciated or even perceived. I don't know how much the nature of it was a function of our youth or our low social status and lack of power—our placement outside of any society but each other—but it was the most meaningful friendship I've had, I think, and the last male friendship of its importance. While in many ways we didn't even like each other. Years later I got a note from Ted Berrigan inviting me to a reading he was giving with Ron Padgett. He wrote that it was the event of the season or something like that and added that he and Ron hated each other as only best friends can. It was the first time I'd seen that syndrome identified, but I knew exactly what he meant, because of Tom and me. The hatred came a little later though. When our friendship was at its most intense, when it was fully active, the hatred was more a kind of tension or confusion, a kind of unease at being a little off balance half the time. We needed each other, and because that made us vulnerable, we resented each other for it, and, after a while, also, just because we'd gotten to know each other so well, we might have despised each other a little. Then there was the unspoken competition going on. This is a particular, atypical type of friendship, but I don't think it's unusual among young artists, at least among egotistical ambitious young artists.

It was in this time, 1971 through 1975, that we settled into the bookstore jobs, the last series of day jobs we would have before becoming professional musicians. Tom had an interesting one for a while with a dealer of books that were translations into English. We discovered a lot of writers because of that, like Albert Cossery (*A Life Full of Holes*), Knut Hamsun (*Hunger*), and the interesting poets Robert Bly translated and published in small editions for his *The Fifties* and then *The Sixties* and then *The Seventies* literary magazines, like George Trakl, Juan Ramón Jiménez, Rumi, and Rilke. We both had jobs at the Strand for a while—me for the second time—though not simultaneously. Our final day jobs were at a specialty bookshop devoted to movies—literature as well as graphics (stills and posters), etc., too—called Cinemabilia, where we did both work at the same time for a while.

We also always read the new books, mostly mimeographed, stapled pamphlets, from the "second generation New York School" poets linked to the St. Mark's Church Poetry Project, which was a block away from Tom's apartment. I was more interested in those guys than Tom was though. He could never accept the low-key, daily, Frank O'Hara chitchat, "I did this, I did that" style they used a lot. We both liked their wise-guy ways and cartooniness and wildness though, and their most abstract stuff. The least-known of our favorites among them was a guy named Tom Veitch, who did actually end up writing for comic books (though dullish sci-fi/fantasy), as well as becoming a cloistered monk for a while—which was probably a side of him Tom could relate to.

Veitch was brilliant and hilarious—he actually tore through the veil by goofing. One of my favorite artifacts of that great American poetry moment is Veitch's *Toad Poems*, a mimeo booklet attributed only to "PSEUDONYM" and introduced by a one-page "Preliminary Toast" from Veitch's good friend Ron Padgett. Padgett wrote, "I've always dreamed of a poetry that would be, without any special connotations to the word, bad, as well as pleasurable," and continued as to how he'd "never read anything so genuinely sub-intelligent and unconcerned, yet perfectly aware of itself" as this book's poetry.

The first poem in it goes:

Cats Climb Trees

Cats climb trees because they are
Afraid of Dogs.
My dog was not afraid of me,
So I never climbed any trees.
Twenty years ago this happened.
Since then my dog has died
and been buried under a tree
in our front yard.
Today I climbed that tree for
the first time, to chase down a
cat named Melvin who had got
caught up there after running
from my new dog whose name
shall not be mentioned
(We call him Ron)
My Sister wrote that.

It's terrible by any standard except one's favored one, by which it is real good. Tom liked Veitch even if he wouldn't class him with Rilke or Rumi. In fact, Tom's own poetry of the time had values not dissimilar to Veitch's. For instance, one of my favorites of Tom's poems I ever saw was an untitled and unparaphraseable two lines about a day's endless sky through his "noses" leaving him breathless and how that must have followed from his cowboyness.

That one I published in *Genesis : Grasp* and had scheduled to appear in a pamphlet of his things I intended to call *Merde*, which I planned for Philosophical Review Editions.

In my memory the entire two or three years of 1971–73, as Tom and I took in everything together and I peaked in poetry and then shifted to rock and roll, happened in springtime. It sounds symbolic, but it's not. It's involuntary. And always in the spring I get transported to that time again for moments. What else do I associate with those days? Tom and I both smoked nonfilter cigarettes, a pack or two a day. A pack cost $0.35 or so. He tended to get Gauloises, while I smoked Lucky Strikes. Sometimes we'd need to roll our own from $0.15 packages of Top or Bugler loose tobacco. Our apartments were bare; we sat on the floor a lot. He mostly wore corduroy jeans or baggy white housepainter's pants, and those big brown wingtip shoes that had been typical in boarding school. We had a lot of T-shirts, including some with horizontal stripes; often they were frayed. We never wore anything ironed. My clothes were a slightly more various mix because I'd had a little financial help from Patty (I even had a suit, a kind of mod one) and I liked to dress fairly deliberately. I'd sometimes find and buy a shirt or pants that had a style I liked because it reminded me of cowboys, or the early Rolling Stones, or Dylan Thomas, or a private eye.

Tom had an old tobacco sunburst flattop Gibson acoustic guitar he'd mess around on for hours most days. He also liked to draw cartoons and wavery shapes and write down little lines of goofiness in notebooks. I kept journals and notebooks. There were always spiral-bound lined-paper notebooks lying around where we lived. We both had cheap portable record players and a few records. Nearly all of what few possessions we had came from the trash and from thrift stores and junk stores and used-book stores.

We were partial to odd little shops run by people who were interested in their own merchandise, the way used-book dealers like Mr. Sackin were. There was a store called Sindoori that we both loved. We always referred to its owner as Sindoori, though eventually we learned that his name was Mr. Green, Peter Green. He imported odds and ends from India, directly, traveling there to find merchandise. When we first discovered his store, it occupied a spacious ground floor on Second Avenue across from St. Mark's Church. As the East Village became more busy, he was forced to move to smaller and smaller rooms further and further from the center of the neighborhood. He was a dignified, quiet, wry, slightly plump white guy, Jewish presumably, in glasses and a kurta, observant amid the inexpensive incense, shirts, pants, and sandals, kohl, Hindu statuettes, religious tracts, jewelry, soap, and brass or carved-and-painted exotic art-trinkets that stuffed the shop. After the place'd moved a couple of times, his latest tiny storefront was so packed there was literally room only for him and at most two skinny others to stand just inside the door among the tottering stacks and overfull shelves. The shop smelled musty and sweet. Everything came in fantastic packaging—crude, matte, colorful, heavily filigreed in calligraphic Indian lettering, all frontier homemade seeming, like the back pages' columns of minuscule advertisements in old pulp magazines; faded and dusty and individual. These things hadn't been expected to get to the United States. They were Eastern; the room was an alley in Bombay.

Tom bought incense there. His favorite was called Heena Agarbatti and came in a foot-long ornately shield-and-curlicue-decorated paper-covered cylindrical cardboard package with a metal cap. He'd burn a stick on his peeling-paint windowsill. Twenty years later I was astonished to discover Sindoori still existed when I chanced on it again in a cubby-hole storefront just one block east of me on Twelfth Street. Mr. Green recognized me immediately and also asked after the friend I was always with. I bought a container of the Heena Agarbatti.

Back in my sunlit living room I burned a stick of that incense, disoriented by the mixture of that day with ones two decades before. I felt incongruous, like a big broken-off piece of furniture or an empty package, mechanically shuttled, as if I was a carnival ride, jerkily but not—because the violence wasn't felt by the rider constituted as the rigid vehicle—across the choppy waves of interim existence to that different time. It was not possible to grasp what was taking place, because I was as much a function of it as I was its observer, but it was very great.

Those days were lush and intense, even though I was frustrated and starved and uncertain. I was open to experience and excited about my own abilities. I was unknown, not publicly respected, but I knew I could see clearly, that I had vision, and I loved the certain poems and songs and cartoons I'd found in those years that were my fetishes and that supported me intellectually and aesthetically and psychologically, along with a particular few of my own ideas and experiences. I was envious of and felt competitive with others who'd already accomplished things, who seemed to be able to express themselves better than me, but I didn't feel inferior to them. I was full of initiative and I was sure I could make happen what I wanted to make happen. I thought that my sensibility was subtle and complex, that it was interesting, and that what excited me in the things I loved existed inside me and that I could find ways to translate that into works that would be as beautiful and thrilling as I wanted.

It was Theresa Stern who first gave me what I regarded as indisputable evidence of this, and it was at this time, when we were both twenty-one, that Tom and I invented her. After we wrote that first "Ode to Mr. Sackin" poem, we kept writing poems together, usually late at night. It's what we did instead of watch TV (we didn't own one) when we were talked out and not wrapped up in reading. For me, it was stimulating. I liked doing it and it gave me thoughts and ideas. I liked the poems too.

We both favored a certain type of surrealist poem—good examples of which had been written by César Vallejo and Bill Knott, for instance—the surrealism of which wasn't purely irrational, but was based in conscious thoughts and feelings and perceptions, while still acknowledging that experience precedes thought, precedes any organization, and is funny. The original, for me, of this was Lautréamont's *Maldoror. Les Chants de Maldoror* was written from 1868 to 1869, when its author, French/Argentine Isidore Ducasse—pen name Le Comte de Lautréamont—was twenty-two to twenty-three. Ducasse died in Paris a year after that, by suicide it's speculated. The book is a rhapsody of evil, of antiromance, reveling in the voice of aggressive disgust with and opposition to life, opposition to all sentimentality and received corny humanist ideas—while still somehow in the service to beauty, in a language and imagery and conceptual framework forced into being by the demands of its new worldview, setting the precedent for surrealism. It's so extreme that it's as funny as it is shocking. *Maldoror* inspired me above all other works for its demonstration of the possibilities of writing, for the way it bypasses convention to speak directly from wild unfiltered vision.

Knott was our most immediate model since he was American and near to our age (about eight years older than us). His first book had come out in 1968, and, so far, all his books had been perfect—delirious in a way consistent with the present, inspired by roots surrealism, they were fully thought-through funny word packs of imagery and ideas of: loneliness, desperate love, shock and fury at general hypocrisy and greed, and pain at American politics and warmongering. Knott was probably the strongest influence on Theresa, but she was more cynically hopeless and mocking than him.

It didn't take many of our collaborations for me to start seeing their potential. Writing collaboratively freed me from inhibitions, and the poems were unlike what we wrote separately, while having a consistent style. I thought they would make a good book, and it would be fun to conceive it as the work of a separate third person. Tom was OK with this idea. He suggested making her a woman. Feminism and androgyny and transvestitism were in the air (Andy Warhol, Mick Jagger, the National Organization for Women). We'd cash in! I started imagining her biography.

Tom was passive about where this went. He could never admit to caring about much that didn't originate with him and often treated anything not in his specific realm as being trivial, even contemptible. This could be maddening, but at the same time I knew the directions I wanted to go with the idea and preferred to be left alone to do it. Tom did usually defer to me as a writer, even if his ego conflicted with that sometimes.

Writing the poems was so much fun. Night after night we'd be up late with maybe a quart of beer, or a fresh-scooped pint of vanilla ice cream from Gem Spa, in Tom's bare rooms, smoking cigarettes and passing the typewriter back and forth.

Tom would get pissed off by the way I'd sabotage a line he'd just written, or when I'd go obnoxious and antipoetic. For instance, to a short poem the fifth line of which, written by Tom, went, "How perfect! I sit in the Holy Fire!" I added, "and in the bowl—alphabet shit, spelling THERESA." I can't remember who wrote which of the previous four lines. The full poem went like this:

> Though human "hands" are scissors
> it's not a question of perception
> but of prehistoric love.
> I'm immortal: too lazy for this planet.
> How perfect! I sit in the Holy Fire! and
>
> in the bowl—
> alphabet shit, spelling THERESA

I called her Theresa Stern with the idea that she had a German Jewish father and a Puerto Rican–American mother (the ethnic/national roots of my father and the largely underprivileged class of my mother), and that she was stern. She came from Hoboken, New Jersey.

Tom and I had once or twice taken day trips to Hoboken, across the Hudson from New York, just out of curiosity—partly because Frank Sinatra came from there—and we liked the place. At that time it was really run-down. It had been a busy port but was neglected and crumbling by then. The abandoned waterfront was overgrown and there were dark rows of derelict piers sticking way out into the water, weighed down by huge decrepit warehouses into which ships' cargoes had once been unloaded. These giant storage sheds were littered with rusty equipment and refuse, like the mammoth mounds of grainy white powder that filled one we explored. Years of stone-throwing trespassers

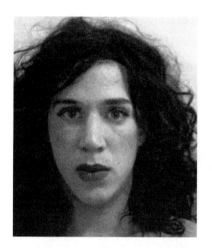 

Her components . . . *Theresa looked a bit hard*

had splintered the tiny grids of windowpanes up near the roofs of the buildings. Once we flushed out a covey of transvestites in the half dark.

So Theresa was a hooker who lived in Hoboken.

I arranged for a friend I'd met at an office job, Charlotte Deutsch, to take pictures for the author's headshot. I got her to put identical makeup on Tom and me, we took turns wearing a big black wig, and she shot us each from exactly the same distance and angle so I could superimpose the negatives for the portrait. Theresa looked a bit hard but unashamed.

I used that photo, along with ones of Rimbaud and Artaud, for the cover of that final issue of *Genesis : Grasp* (number 5/6). Once I had Theresa's manuscript together I decided to pose as her literary agent and submit the book to big publishers. They all turned it down. A couple of years later, in 1973, I published it myself in a new series of poetry pamphlets called Dot Books.

ndrew Wylie had rented a tiny storefront on Jones Street between Bleecker and West Fourth in the West Village and had set up shop as Telegraph Books. At the front of the room were a few shelves with books of poetry for sale, and at the back was a mattress where he slept. In 1971, shortly after it opened, I came across the place and stepped inside and we started talking. His real mission was the series of poetry pamphlets he was publishing. He was a poet who had a lot of ideas about how poems should be promoted.

He had two partners in Telegraph Books—Victor Bockris, an unsmiling, brisk, talkative little British guy, and Aram Saroyan, whom I never met but knew of from his writing. Saroyan was an inspired, advanced, and relatively widely published poet in his late twenties. He was the oldest of the three and the only one of them with a reputation. Wylie had just recently come down to New York from college at Harvard and was two or three years older than me. Bockris was about my age. I didn't cross paths with him more than once or twice back then. He lived in Philadelphia.*

---

* Wylie has since become the reputed "jackal" of literary-world fame, for his matchless success as a writers' agent of ruthless initiative. His Wylie Agency represents half the bestselling first-rate writers on earth. Bockris is a journal-

Andrew always dressed in a black leather motorcycle jacket and a beret—he was balding—and was an aggressive, wired street person, who was also charming, a joker. He was a born salesman. Pretty soon I realized that he came from a wealthy family, but his gutter style still seemed genuine. I remember he said he'd spent time in a mental hospital. He was short and skinny and pale, with a face like a shaved pug dog starved to the point of transparency. In canine spirit he was more like a pit bull though, with the energy level of a Chihuahua. He liked amphetamines. His voice sounded just like John Malkovich's and he gave that same impression of being smart and a jump ahead that Malkovich does. Always a little snort smirk laugh.

He was an "alpha" personality. He was always "on" and always had to be on top, one-upping everyone in the vicinity. He never showed self-doubt and he crackled with tactics for domination. This didn't mean he was unlikable. He was ahead of you even in anticipating your fatigue with him, and would then get humble. He was funny and generous and encouraging, even if it was calculated. He and Bockris in their later incarnation as Bockris-Wylie, a poetry-writing, interview-conducting literary/journalistic team, consciously strove to gain sympathy and cooperation from their subjects by making them "feel good about themselves" via strategic flattery.

Andrew's main model was Andy Warhol, because of Warhol's combination of artistic talent with overriding worldly ambition and the marketing savvy to fulfill that ambition. Andrew was discriminating—he may have been tightly wound to succeed, but it was in the service of the most interesting art, or at least the most interesting art

---

ist specializing in assembly-line biographies of successful, relatively "high-art" practitioners of popular culture, like Patti Smith and Keith Richards and Andy Warhol. Saroyan is a benevolent literary scholar, poet, and writing teacher.

that he could imagine being profitable. His ceaseless competitive drive could be maddening, but I almost felt sorry for him. It was lonely work and hard work keeping everyone conscious that he was ahead of them.

As a poet he was into sex and violence. He was aware that these subjects sold, but it's true as well that they sell because they fascinate and excite people, and Andrew was a person, so it was only natural that they excited him too. I liked his poems. They were highly influenced by Aram Saroyan's minimalist style as well as by Giuseppe Ungaretti (Wylie had edited a special issue of the British literary magazine *Agenda* in 1970 that was entirely devoted to Ungaretti, and Andrew had translated a majority of the many poems in it). Here are a few of my favorites of his:

> I'm a
> tramp
>
> —
>
> a trap
>
> —
>
> I'm a
> trap

and

> lie down
> in yellow
> flowers
>
> it's the whole
> world

and

I fuck
your
ass

you suck
my cock

He had a flair. With Telegraph he wanted to make poetry as popular as rock and roll and movies, and make poets stars. The style of the books owed a lot to the City Lights Pocket Poets series. They were small and simply designed in a uniform format. One difference from the Pocket Poets books though was that Andrew's books had a black-and-white film-studio-style glamour shot of each book's author on its front cover, like a rock album. The books were brief and so were most of the individual poems—they had a "telegraphic" style that way.

His belief in the potential of poetry to excite mass appeal, and his intention to nakedly work to make that happen, was just what I needed to hear about at that moment.

I made a book by Andrew the first in my new publishing venture, Dot Books. It was Andrew's idea to model the book's appearance on mass-market paperbacks. We printed the book at that standard size and with a glossy cover and other signifiers indicating it belonged on a rack in a drugstore or an airport, rather than in a literary bookstore where it'd be hidden in the back with the other small-press consignments. In 1972 and 1973 I planned and gathered the material for four more in this series: Theresa's *Wanna Go Out?*, Tom's *21st Century* (which I'd renamed from my original title for it, *Merde*), Patti Smith's *Merde* (I thought the title was too good to go to waste, so to speak), and *The Voidoid* by me.

I can't remember how I first heard about Patti Smith. Between 1971 and '73 I saw her acting in a play (*Island* by Tony Ingrassia), and I saw her read at the gay nightclub Le Jardin, and at the Poetry Project at St. Mark's Church, which was one of the first times she ever sang, and was definitely the first time she had musical accompaniment to her singing—she ended the poetry reading by having Lenny Kaye play guitar for her on one or two pieces of writing. I also saw her read as an opening act for the New York Dolls at the Mercer Arts Center. The St. Mark's musical interlude was as elaborate as her singing got until after she came to see Television play at CBGB in early 1974, when she started forming a full band.

Tom was with me for at least one of those Patti appearances, possibly all four. Her first book, *Seventh Heaven*, was published by Wylie on Telegraph in 1972. It was frighteningly new and good, and so were her performances. She fulfilled Andrew's demand for an electrifying, rock-and-roll-level poetry. Patti was triply stunning at that time, not only because her stuff was hair-raising on the page, but because her performances were so seductive and funny and charismatic that the writing was lifted way beyond the page, and then, third, she was self-possessed and plugged in to the point that she would improvise and riff extensions as she read, like a bebop soloist or an action painter, off to a whole other plane beyond the beyond. She was a natural-born sex waif and a pretty-assed comedian. She'd step out with her hand on her tight-cocked hip, all casual, if in-your-face, and jack out mind and body gush, giggling at herself like a five-year-old, under her deep-set eyes and her coal-black shag, begging to be fucked, skinny as a rod, massive tits deceptively draped in her threadbare overlarge Triumph motorcycles T-shirt, and then twirl away, denying you in favor of Anita Pallenberg.

At the same time as I was working up the Dot Books series, the New York Dolls were taking off. Tom and I went to a couple of their shows at the Mercer Arts Center. We saw them headlining above the Modern Lovers, and also with Patti Smith opening, still only speaking, though she fooled with a little toy piano onstage at that gig. The Dolls were as riveting as Patti, and their music, though simple and sloppy, was physically thrilling. Their gigs were unlike any I'd ever experienced. They were parties, they were physical orgies, without much distinc-tion between the crowd and the band: the band felt like an expres-sion of the dressed-up avant-garde teenagers, and all the downtown hipster cognoscenti who'd materialized from the gutter glitter of the whole sexy area and history itself. It was like some kind of funny dirty religious revel. The band was theatrical and mocking, self-mocking—semicamp, like a bright crumpled-tissue gift presentation of the weird thing inside. As it turned out, you kind of "had to be there"—the effect didn't really translate either to record or to concert hall. Its habitat was downtown New York clubs and it didn't survive transplanting.

In 1972 Tom and I were following what was going on in New York and England in music and I started getting the idea we should form a band. I knew I could do it and I saw how I could use my chops as a writer, and my perception of what was interesting to do in rock and roll, as a songwriter, onstage, and in the whole arena (singing, clothes, haircuts, names, posters, interviews, etc.). I was a little nervous about not knowing how to play any instrument, but Tom said it was easy to play bass for the kind of music we wanted to do.

ven though Tom imagined his future as a professional singer-songwriter, he never did anything about it except to continuously mess around on his acoustic guitar, sketch out a few folkie songs, and once or twice a year go to an open-mike night at a folk club. I can kind of understand that, or think I understand it. It was a form of egotism, like my refusal to try to get accepted by the groups of poets in New York I admired. It would have been humiliating to present myself for approval. We knew we were good and we didn't have anything to prove. On the other hand I've always been interested in making things happen. My inclination is to put it out there and see where it leads. But Tom was too proud, at least at first, until I suggested we team up and go electric.

He found me a copper-colored, little lightweight $50 used Danelectro bass and we started rehearsing quietly in his apartment, practicing the three or four keeper songs he'd written. At the same time I started working on lyrics and melodies to some guitar compositions he'd got going that he hadn't worked up words for. The idea was that he'd sing his lyrics and I'd sing mine, and eventually I'd write music too. I had the name for the group: the Neon Boys.

We were going to supersede the new "glamour" bands whose music we liked, such as the Dolls and Iggy and Slade and T. Rex. We

Preliminary Neon Boys.

were into that driving, crazed, riff-strong music, like what was made in the midsixties by the early Stones, electric Dylan, the Standells, the Seeds, the Kingsmen, etc. The hard-pumping 1972 platform-shoe, eye-makeup, and wack hair groups were a welcome replacement for the horrible symphonic-rock and bloated arena muck ruining American radio at the time, but Tom and I were different, and we wanted to strip everything down further, away from the showbiz theatricality of the glitter bands, and away from bluesiness and boogie. We wanted to be stark and hard and torn up, the way the world was.

Already there was a split between us though. Tom didn't like the Dolls. He liked Jonathan Richman and the Modern Lovers more.

Richman was an idiot savant of a Velvet Underground–besotted nerdy rock and roller. Like Tom, he had a vision that was personal and that he stubbornly, insistently purveyed as a magic territory in the world, musical and otherwise. He cultivated, and sheltered himself in, a wide-eyed, if intelligent, American-reality-embracing childishness. "I'm in love with the modern world," he sang. "Roadrunner, a thousand miles an hour," driving past the malls, into the nightways. I liked Richman too but found the Dolls more exciting and interesting. Tom was a reserved, wound-up person, and the Dolls were too loose for him. It was the same as in poetry—he had problems with Frank O'Hara because too much was allowed in Frank O'Hara. That flamboyance made Tom uncomfortable and made him feel threatened; at least that's my interpretation.

Tom was highly protected, well defended. There are good things and bad things about that. It gave him a certain kind of integrity—he wasn't going to be blown around by fashion, he was discreet and reliable, but it made him really difficult to work with or be friends with. He was afraid of infection and robbery, so he lived in this high, remote, walled-in place, which enabled him to look down on everybody else. To me, extremes like that always suggest the presence of their opposites—in other words that somehow, somewhere, he must have been very insecure to need to be so heavily defended. But he never showed the insecurity. On the contrary, he showed nothing but contempt for any activity at which he didn't believe himself to be adept. Things were only interesting to him that were either completely innocent (cartoons)—and by that token nonthreatening—or that existed in a realm where he felt supremely capable (like highly constructed, technically proficient, emotionally strong guitar playing). Over and over again I experienced his scorn for, or conspicuous indifference to, my interest in things that weren't his forte. I respected his abilities and valued his friendship, but his coldness and egotism came more and more to the fore as he began to get more public attention. He was a lot easier to get along with before strangers started admiring him.

At the beginning, though, our collaboration was complete and balanced. Naturally I deferred to Tom in musical matters at the start, but we had the same aims and values, musical and otherwise, for the band anyway, so there was no issue. And my lyrics and vocal delivery were just as strong as his. I was writing a lot of songs: "Love Comes in Spurts," "Change Your Channel," "Eat the Light," "I'm Nice," "That's All I Know (Right Now)," "High Heel Wheels"— which was the first and only one of these to which I wrote the music (its attitude was influenced by Marc Bolan—Tom and I both appreciated Bolan, digging the *Slider* LP for instance)—and "Blank Generation," etc.

After a few months, once we'd gotten six or seven songs well rehearsed, Tom contacted a drummer friend of his from Delaware, Billy Ficca, with whom he'd had a short-lived band in high school. Ficca, who had an unusual, spiky, stop-and-start free-jazz playing style, agreed to come to New York to rehearse with us in anticipation of finding the second guitar player we'd need to start playing shows.

We put an ad in the *Village Voice* classifieds that read, "Narcissistic rhythm guitarist wanted—minimal talent okay."

We wanted someone who would be interesting to look at, not be completely stupid, have a reasonable command of guitar basics, and be willing to play the parts Tom would teach him. We did also want him to be at least a little simpatico with us in character and taste. We had no luck with it though.

Among the guitarists who came over to Tom's apartment and auditioned for us were Doug Colvin, who'd soon be Dee Dee Ramone, and

Chris Stein, who would be the guitarist, songwriter, and musical direc-tor of Blondie (and longtime boyfriend of Debbie Harry).

Dee Dee was a riot. He could only play barre chords—that's the single frozen, clawlike fingering that is simply clamped up and down the guitar neck to produce a common chord at any fret. To get started we told Dee Dee that the song we'd try out would be in the key of C. So he put barre chord fingering at a position on the neck, and we had to shake our heads, "No—C." He slid the fingering to another fret. We shook our heads. He looked up quizzically, puppyish, eager to please, with that shining hair of his and friendly grin. Again, wrong. I al-ways liked Dee Dee. We would become extra-good friends for a while a couple of years later.

Probably the problem with Chris was that he was too mellow and had hippie hair and wore glasses. I always liked him, too, though.

The three-fourths Neon Boys continued for months, rehearsing while searching for a second guitarist, Tom and I both working full-time. Ficca made a lot of sacrifices, staying in Tom's tiny apartment with him, unable to earn any money. As I recall, he got a job as a messenger for a little while. Finally we had to give up and let him return to Delaware. Before he left though, we salvaged something from all our efforts by recording a few of the songs we'd worked up. From out of the *Voice* classifieds we found a four-track room in a guy's basement in Queens and laid down three of Tom's songs, "Hot Dog," "Poor Circulation," and either "Bluebird" or "$16.50," I believe, and three of mine, "Love Comes in Spurts," "That's All I Know (Right Now)" (both of which were Tom's guitar compositions with my lyrics and singing), and "High Heel Wheels." Tom has never let his material from those days be heard. The songs of mine are typi-cal of what we sounded like at the time though, and what Television sounded like at the beginning: driving, angry, ecstatic übermodern rock and roll.

In person, we were also at the state that we'd bring public with Television a year or so later. We'd cut our hair short and ragged. I did mine in a style that poked up in shreds and thatches all over my skull. Our clothes were torn and frayed and sometimes held together by safety pins. I often wore a wrinkled baggy suit and an old tie that was pulled loose down my shirtfront. At other times I wore a leather jacket—not a motorcycle jacket, which I considered trite, but a policeman's jacket, bought at a policeman's supply shop near the police academy. (I tried to get Tom to get some police clothes too, which is where those lines in one of his songs comes from, "Richard said, hey let's dress up like cops, but something in me said I'd better not," or something like that.) I wore sunglasses a lot too, but never Ray-Bans, which I also thought were clichéd. I liked round, horn-rimmed dark glasses, like Ivy League gone depraved or early Andy Warhol.

My style was deliberately calculated. I wore pegged black jeans. Before I did that, no one on the street wore anything but blue denim jeans. Black ones were hard to find. I was able to find only one store in the entire city that carried them. (Further sartorial anecdote: Once Television got popular and our social circle started expanding, I became friends with Barbara Troiani, a great girl who made a lot of clothes for the Dolls. I showed her a Wilson Pickett album cover and asked her for a suit in purple sharkskin that was cut like that. I loved that suit. It's the remnants of its jacket I'm holding open on the cover of *Blank Generation*.)

None of this clothing cost anything much, which was part of the point. It was an alternative to the international stadium jet-set superstar queens who'd stolen rock and roll and spoiled it. Part of what excited me about rock and roll was all the languages of it, clothes and hair most definitely included. You could subvert certain aspects of its signifying potential while indulging in others.

I arrived at the haircut by analysis. Rock and roll had had two main innovative hairstyles so far: the Elvis ducktail, and the Beatles bowl cut. I tried to figure out what they signified and what they had in common and what made them work. Elvis's more or less had already existed—its power was in its southern underclass hoodlum origin (along with the reverse-machismo of the way it required so much attention to maintain, and in that way screamed vanity), and the shock of that suddenly being splashed as glamorous and successful onto the front pages of national music magazines and then newspapers, when before it'd been limited to mug shots—truck drivers and bootleggers and petty thieves.

The Beatles' haircut, on the other hand, had been created by the band. It said two interesting, conflicting things: one was innocence and youthful charm, since it was a hairstyle typical of five-year-olds of the Beatles' generation, and two was perversion, transgression, and defiance, since among adults only girls or bohemian freaks and artists wore their hair that long.

I thought of what the haircut of my childhood had been, and it was a super-short, stiff, almost military "butch" or "crew" cut that had gone ragged because kids don't like going to barbers. When that patchy raggedness was exaggerated to the degree that I exaggerated it, it expressed defiance and criminality too. For one thing, a guy with a haircut like that couldn't have an office job. In addition, it didn't require a barber. In fact no barber could even conceive of it. It was something you had to do yourself, and something that flaunted its freedom from propriety, even from stylishness.

I also came at the clothes a few ways, which were related to the haircut. I liked cowboys, I liked private detectives, I liked the ghetto rags the Bowery Boys wore in *Dead End* (as I'd first seen in all the great comedy shorts with Leo Gorcey and Huntz Hall that were replayed constantly on TV in New York in the sixties and seventies). I liked the dandyism of the early Rolling Stones, too.

But it was also important that it all be easy to do for nothing, from thrift shops and work-clothes purveyors. One strategy I used was to wear articles of clothing that had evolved for the use of people whose profession relied on the high functionality of the given piece of clothing—in the way that blue jeans were originally frontier work clothes. I got my shoes from tap-shoe makers (not Capezio) and that leather jacket from a police store. For the Voidoids' first gig, I dressed us in baggy, boxy black corduroy workingman's suits from Hudson's huge work-clothes emporium on Thirteenth Street and Third Avenue. They cost $50 each and they looked great and were fantastically comfortable.

It was also important that the band's stage clothes and their street clothes be the same. We were ourselves as performers, not just a show business act, even though our stage appearances were violent and drunken and crazed. Probably the major, overriding thrust of everything I wanted to do in rock and roll was to bring real life back into it. I played this up by favoring torn clothes, and by sometimes reconstructing them with safety pins to make sure the point couldn't be missed.

There are some misconceptions about the origins of the hairstyle and torn clothes that have gotten a lot of play in punk journalism. It's often said that I based my haircut on Rimbaud. Probably that comes from an interview I did once in which I mentioned that a year or two after I started the hairstyle I noticed that the cover of the final issue of my literary magazine (1971) features pictures of two guys with similar hair: Rimbaud and Artaud. And that that had reminded me of another example: the Jean-Pierre Léaud of *The 400 Blows* (who's actually an

The Neon Boys ready to rumble.

example of the 1950s kid's-hair look that my reasoning had arrived at). But noticing those was after the fact, though who knows whether there might have been some influence. The other is a weird false anecdote that all my clothes were torn because an angry girlfriend had done that to my wardrobe and I couldn't afford new clothes. That didn't happen. It's the kind of thing punk interviewees like to say to sound "insider" savvy. It's obvious from all the publicity pictures I oversaw from 1974 on that I was deliberately proposing torn togs.

And then there were our names. While everything else about how we conceived the band had meaning and purpose, our names sounded hopelessly banal: Tom Miller and Richard Meyers. I decided on Hell pretty quickly. I liked it as soon as I thought of it. It was assertive but

I DREAMED I WAS A VERY CLEAN TRAMP

negative without being too specific, and it captured my condition. Coming up with something for Tom was harder. Then I thought of copping the name of a nineteenth-century French poet. Right away that seemed correct. I suggested Gautier, thinking it should not be a poet who was too well known because that would come off as pretentious and literary. Then immediately I realized Gautier wouldn't work because there'd be problems with its pronunciation. Tom came back with "Verlaine" and that sounded perfect. It was musical, and though the poet wasn't known to most Americans, his writing was exquisitely lyrical—all full of autumn and violins and wistful, if sensual, love— while also simple and straightforward (including some pornography), and he was an archetypal bohemian mess. Of course I was conscious of the Rimbaldian tinge "Hell" might carry, especially juxtaposed with "Verlaine," but what the hell. It was settled: Verlaine and Hell.

The whole process of reconceiving ourselves as a band was interesting and satisfying. It hadn't occurred to me before how all-encompassing a self-invention or self-realization making a band could be, but the moment I began picturing myself in music, I understood. (Doubtless David Bowie was a signpost too, though I wasn't a fan of his. He seemed too artificial to me.) There was much more to having a band than writing and performing songs, and instantly I felt like I was in my element—that I could do this in a way that had hardly ever been done before, because it felt natural to me.

Eventually, this would be part of what separated Tom and me and what made it impossible for us to work together, but at the beginning, it was different—he appreciated and accepted my conception of the band as a subculture.

Sadly, all these ideas had to be left half-realized though, when the band project had to be set aside because our search for a guitarist had failed.

CHAPTER FOURTEEN

A̲t this time, towards the middle of 1973, I met Andrew's sister, Jennifer Wylie, and we started going out. She was nineteen, with blond hair, a creamy complexion, and a ruled profile like a Greek statue. She was ample without being overweight, also like Aphrodite. She had a surface toughness that she copped from her older brother's hardass ways, but underneath she was sweet and kind and a little uncertain. As a Wylie, she had enough money to live decently without having to work. She got an apartment in a renovated building that overlooked the old graveyard in the west yard of St. Mark's Church and I spent most nights at her place for a while.

While the band was on hold I started writing a piece of fiction. A couple of the old buildings on Jennifer's pretty, tree-lined street— probably the most genteel block in the East Village—were anomalous for having been converted to cheap SRO fleabags. You wouldn't know it from the street except that the buildings' windows were filthy and some of them had milk cartons and cold cuts on their ledges in winter, meaning no refrigerators there. I rented a room in one to use for writing. At $16 a week it came with a cot, a dresser, a night table, and a kitchen chair; the bathroom was in the hall. The little bed took up over half the floor space. The window looked out onto Tenth Street from the third floor. I brought in a typewriter and a portable record player, and every day I'd go spend a few hours there working on the book. The rooms were so shabby you could slip the lock on a door with a piece of cardboard, so I took a hammer to the case of my little blue Olivetti to discourage theft.

I kept two record albums there, which I'd rotate nonstop while I was writing—the Who's *My Generation* and James Brown's *Live at the Apollo*. The other part of my routine was that I'd bring a cheap bottle of red wine to drink as I wrote. I wouldn't stop typing until I'd covered one single-spaced page per visit, and I'd quit there, usually in the middle of a sentence. That made it easy to pick up where I'd left off. I think I got this trick from an Ernest Hemingway interview.

The book in progress was called *The Voidoid*. That word was born over payday fat burgers and steak-cut fries with Tom at the Second Avenue Deli. I said he could be described by attaching "-oid" to any noun and we started calling each other this-and-that-oid. Eventually he called me voidoid. I ran with it.

The book riffs on life as I knew it at the time. In it, I'm "Arthur Black" and Tom is "Caspar Skull" and we're known as "Lips" and "Skull." Lips, the title character, is a somewhat sympathetic vampire. Lips and Skull have a band called the Liberteens. Jennifer shows up in it. ("My thoughts and me are like ships that pass in the night," as she'd actually said.) All the locations are real (Tom's apartment, my apartment, the Lower East Side, Hoboken). Andrew is president Booko Wooko (the double o's pronounced as in "boo!"). Theresa gets a whole chapter.

It was influenced by *Maldoror*. When I decided I was done with it, I typed a clean copy, using a fresh ribbon, on deluxe rag paper, in single-spaced lines but with extra-wide margins all around, so that each page was a rectangular black slab of glyphs inside wide white borders, the way the New Directions edition of *Maldoror* looked. I sealed the typescript with a title page on which I carefully centered my thumbprint in blood.

At around this time I started working at Cinemabilia, my final and best day job. The shop, at Thirteenth Street just west of Fifth Avenue, was easy walking distance from wherever I would sleep (my apartment, Tom's apartment, Jennifer's apartment). The work was a breeze while being interesting and educational, and I was appreciated by the management. The pay was almost nothing, but it cost almost nothing to live in New York at that time, if your needs were few, as mine were.

The management comprised two people—the owner of the store, Ernest Burns, who was there all day most days, and his lieutenant, Terry Ork, the nominal manager, who knew the stock almost as well as Mr. Burns, and who wrangled the register. Both of them knew their film, but Mr. Burns specialized in Hollywood, while Terry had mastered the rest of world cinema, especially European—the French New Wave and Godard in particular.

I can't say exactly how much I knew and thought about movies before I started working there, but I knew a lot more by the time I left. Before I worked there I liked to read Andrew Sarris's influential film column in the *Village Voice*; by the time I quit, I was making extra cash writing papers for his Columbia University film students ($75 for a guaranteed B+ or better).

I grew up on movies, but in the sixties and seventies film influence was at its height in the world, and movies from all film history and half the globe routinely played in New York. (I also gradually realized that one could argue that cinema had crested fifty years earlier, before sound had distracted attention from its essence. This at the same time that I was finding out that rock and roll had peaked in the fifties, before the Beatles homogenized and corrupted everything.)

Mr. Burns was a big bearlike guy in his early thirties, with a full mustache, a greasy pageboy, and an erect posture, who often pursed his lips and gestured by flipping a hand from the wrist. His default mode was glum impatience, but that was deceptive—he gave gruff, apologetic respect to the knowledgeable. I started off wrapping mail orders, as I'd done at the Strand. Eventually, having learned enough to figure out what photographs from what movies might meet the shyest customer's personal needs, I worked the stills desk.

Tom and I were vaguely aware of Terry Ork from Max's Kansas City. He was five or six years older than us and the most gregarious guy I'd ever known. He was always grinning psychedelically through the beard scruff on his chipmunk cheeks. Everything he said was something he gave you the option of taking as a joke. He was short and chubby, with a weird walk that pressed together his sausage thighs, as he rolled from side to side, while below the knees he was pigeon-toed. It was the walk of a guy actually much fatter than he was. He wore thick plastic teardrop-shaped glasses or tinted round ones, and a big Afro-style haze of frizzy curls. He called everybody "Dog."

His legal name was William Terry, and he had a shady history. There'd been a small scandal when it was discovered that he'd conspired with Gerard Malanga to print and sell some Warhol silk screens without Warhol's knowledge. Malanga was Warhol's assistant. Terry was also privy to local narcotics supplies. He used to cop from this huge black ex-con with abscess-swollen whale-sized forearms, who loved to sit in his dark cold dump on First Avenue and growl his jabber on and on to the genuinely appreciative Ork. An interesting thing, too, which I only found out quite a bit later, was that Bill Knott had dedicated his first book, the amazing *Naomi Poems,* to Terry. They'd been friends and roommates when Knott lived for a short period in New York in the midsixties.

Terry Ork.

Ork was a connoisseur of boys and movies and modern French art and thought, especially the situationists and Godard. He would end up sponsoring my first bands and me, ostensibly as our manager and/ or record label owner. It seems unlikely that the two management figures associated with the first bands of modern "punk"—Malcolm McLaren with the Sex Pistols et cetera, and Terry with Television and the Voidoids et cetera—one British and the other American, should both, independently, consider themselves to be in the lineage of Guy Debord, but it's true.

The difference between them was that McLaren was driven, skilled, and full of brilliant ideas. Terry was a nice guy and a generous guy with advanced taste, but he was all front as a band manager. He had no executive or negotiating abilities and no real vision or drive. He just liked having good-looking boys around and liked getting high and chatting in fake French-intellectual. The band—Television, once it formed out of the dormant Neon Boys in late 1973—granted him the honorary term "manager" in exchange for equipment he bought us and for providing us rehearsal space and acting as our mouthpiece.

I lost patience with him pretty often. When I caught him making no sense, he might act like it was really Dada he was doing, not philosophy. And ultimately he didn't take offense when a listener didn't buy his line. It was all in the service of getting high and finding boys who'd let him enjoy them. This is how we got a second guitar player, Richard Lloyd, enabling the formation of Television: it was a favor Ork could do for that pouty, bleach-blond boy he wanted to keep grateful and indebted to him, and to allow him to keep doing things with his body.

In a common New York syndrome, Terry conceived of himself as an artist even though he didn't produce any work to speak of. But Terry was different because his goodwill and taste were as important as other artists' actual work.

CHAPTER FIFTEEN

A t our first band meeting, at the end of 1973, I brought in a list of potential band names. ("The Neon Boys," with its history, seemed outdated now.) One of them was Television. Tom, with rare volition, preferred that one, and everyone else was OK with it. Much later I noticed that "TV" was his initials.

We rehearsed where Ork lived, in a large loft down in Chinatown, on East Broadway. At one end of it Terry had partitioned off a sort of living room, with a mattress or two in it and some rickety chairs and a little black and white TV. The other end of the loft was all open space, decorated by lobby cards for Bertolucci's *The Conformist,* a pair of white jockey shorts hanging from a nail, and a photo-poster of a full-frontal-nude Iggy Pop. The floor was polished wood but otherwise the loft was industrial, with grubby whitewashed brick walls, heavy security hardware at the windows and door, and a stamped tin ceiling. We set up three mikes and a drum kit and brought in little amps.

The truth of our invention of our songs and our band preceded and transcended all the contentious opinions and stress and competitive junk that kept arising in the band, and that truth was the hilarious, incomparable intoxication of materializing into being these previously nonexistent patterns of sound and meaning and physical motion. It was as fraught and sublime as great Renaissance religious painting; Bellini's *St. Francis* . . .

The power and beauty of it was unimaginable until then. It can't be overstated, that initial rush of realizing, of experiencing, what's possible as you're standing there in the rehearsal room with your guitars and the mikes turned on and when you make a move this physical information comes pouring out and you can do or say anything with it.

It was like having magic powers. The ability to create action at a distance. The sounds that came from the amplifiers were absurdly moving and strange, the variety of them so wide in view of the fact that they came from flicks of our fingers and from our vocal noises, and the way that it was a single thing, an entity, that was produced by the simultaneous reactive interplay of the four band members combining various of their faculties. We were turned into a sound, a flow of sound. I remember having a moment of weird revelation once, that each moment of a phonograph record being played, each millimeter of information conveyed via the needle to the amplifier to the speaker to the ear, is one sound. A whole orchestra is one sound, altering moment by moment, no matter how many instruments go into producing it. And, as our band rehearsed, in each moment we made the sound spray out in arrays we could instantly alter, emanating from inside us and our interplay and our inner beings combined, playing. And the sound included words.

All through this book I've had to search for different ways to say "thrill," "exhilaration," "ecstatic" to communicate particular experiences. Maybe the most extreme example of this class of moment is what I'm trying to describe here. What it felt like to first be creating electrically amplified songs. It was like being born. It was everything one wants from so-called God. The joy of it, the instant inherent awareness that you could go anywhere you wanted with it and everywhere was fascinatingly new and ridiculously effective. It was like making emotion and thought physical, to be undergone apart from oneself.

That's what makes the very beginning then in 1973 and 1974 different, and, in a way, more valuable than anything that came later in my music career, despite its shortcomings and problems and difficulties. It's that it was fresh and every moment had that surging astonishment and pleasure—even if in the service of anger and disgust, as it often was—of anything being possible to make happen. It was like creating the world, and the feeling could never quite happen again, or be sustained, anyway, because familiarity and habit take the edge off.

Narcotics. I'd consumed that codeine cough syrup in high school now and then for a few weeks, and then I'd gone through a phase in the early seventies, when I was living with Jennifer, of occasionally buying it at the drugstore. In those days Romilar off the shelf had a little codeine in it. I'd drink a bottle alone in my Voidoid office as a kind of treat for myself sometimes, but the experience was mixed—grimacing down that thick red syrup by the bottleful; the stunned high, half like you'd got slapped upside the head; the hangover—too much to repeat too often. It was like a McDonald's hamburger—tempting enough that you had to try it again now and then to remind yourself why you didn't do it more often. I didn't have the money to throw away either.

Tom and I, partly out of interest in William Burroughs and Lou Reed, were curious about heroin, but we didn't know anything about finding it. We got lucky once and copped a couple of bags, but it made us both so sick, vomiting, that it destroyed most of our interest. (Also discouraging Tom was the fact that his fraternal twin brother, John, had died from an overdose.)

Ork liked to do heroin like he was having a tea party. He'd make arrangements in advance every couple of weeks, invite three or four friends, and everybody would ritually, fraternally, shoot each other up in his back room. Pretty soon I was included. Once I'd found my level, I was all in. I marveled at the way a nod was like the dream of a dream, a dream you could manipulate—in other words, paradise on earth.

I also usually drank while rehearsing—beer often, sometimes wine, every once in a while a half pint of cheap Wilson's whiskey. Lloyd drank all the time and did dope too. Verlaine and Ficca were straight.

Rock and roll was a way of life. The songs were like the souvenirs or the by-product of that way of life. To choose rock and roll was to reject growing up and reject straight society, and to affirm other ways of being and of looking at the world. I had thought it through and wanted to make our band up from scratch in accordance with what was interesting. Sure, to play in a band was to love music: music in the service of what rock and roll enables.

Rehearsals were parties and cell meetings and cathartic releases. They were about expressing a spirit, an attitude, as much as about detailing musical parts—the attitude and the music were inseparable. I wasn't a bass player, even in strictly musical terms. I was a singer and songwriter who, for convenience, played the songs' bass lines. In the Neon Boys, this worked. But once another guitar player was added, the power shifted to Verlaine and he liked that. Lloyd was a stray dog, following Verlaine for his chance. He was a smart enough guitar player to recognize his dependence on Tom. Tom created all the guitar parts. Lloyd was a sycophant who'd throw a tantrum and whine and pout up to the point where there might really be a crisis and then revert to his default submission to Tom.

There are videotapes of Television rehearsals in 1974 that confirm all this. One excruciating example shows Tom teaching me the bass part to his "Venus de Milo." I'm proud of the command of the bass I exhibit in that clip. I'd been playing bass for six months, whereas Tom had been playing guitar for nine years. I'm managing well. I sound good. But Tom is treating me as if I were a moron, barely suppressing his disgust, clenching his jaw, tightening his lips, rolling his eyes, sighing and flittering with a saintly patience that would be rampaging rage in a lesser soul.

Meanwhile a hungover Richard Lloyd sulks and whines, all petulant, offscreen, refusing to do any work.

On the same tape, modern punk can be seen first emerging, fresh from the conditions, in a couple of full-blown performances: four pathologically skinny guys in ripped shirts, tight black and blue jeans, and spiky short hair blasting their brains out as they slink and drop and quiver around, kicking and bouncing off each other and wrenching their guitars in the service of compelling, noisy, contemptuous, angry, but also lyrical, rock and roll.

These unreleased rehearsal videos, which have circulated among collectors for years, and the three released recordings of Neon Boys songs, and then four or five songs on a couple of early bootleg tapes of live Television shows, are the only evidence of what the group was like when it first got attention at CBGB in the spring of 1974. It was not like the Television on the album that was released in late 1977. In early 1974 we were dressed in cheap black leather (before the Ramones) and torn shirts stuck together with safety pins, thrift-store suits, sunglasses, and sneers and throwaway grins and short hair, and when we played it was like a rolling, tumbling clatter of renegade scrap that was also pretty and heartrending, as if you were seeing it from a distance. It moved you and shook you and woke you up.

But that fresh clatter and bruised flash died as soon as it came to be, like Elvis's twin, as our first gig illustrates.

For weeks I'd been swallowing my pride, enduring Tom's grand-standing jaw-clenches of inhuman patience, in the confidence that it would all come out in the wash of real gigging, of public response.

Ork had already had a few people down to the loft to see us play and so we were able to use some quotes on the poster I made for our debut:

"Killers. Sharp as tacks . . . They made me cry."
—Scott Cohen, *Interview*
"They're finally here—in full pathological innocence . . .
Color, skin, guitars: 'Love in Spurts,' 'Eat the Light,' 'Enfant
Terrible.'"
—Danny Fields, *Sixteen*
"Four cats with a passion."
—Nicholas Ray, director, *Rebel Without a Cause*

Danny had visited the loft and had liked us and just told us to write his. Scott Cohen's was perfect. Nick Ray, the great film director, leftist, and amphetamine head, had watched us rehearse a couple of times.

Beneath our sullen photo on the poster were two lines from the version of "Love Comes in Spurts" we were doing:

Love'll come pump in your soul two feet deep
Two minutes later alligators'll chew you in your sleep

The original conception of the band still held well enough for it to be possible to use my lyrics on the poster. Tom would soon be acting so globally sour that I knew I had to placate him with other empha-ses in the promo. The poster was like a combination mug shot and cheap boxing-match poster. My ideal of the way to present us live was boxing-ring style—a stage like a platform, a boxing ring, on which we

In full pathological innocence . . . Poster photo for first
Television show, Townhouse Theater, New York City, 1974.

performed in white light against the crowd-walls. No pomp or special
effects, just the high-lit band, swinging and bleeding and crying and
sneering.

Terry had rented a screening room in midtown, the Townhouse
Theater, for our first date. It held about two hundred people. My idea
for ramping up our presentation was to place four or five televisions
onstage. During our performance each was tuned to a different channel, while one of them was hooked up to the Portapak of the video guy
who'd been taping our rehearsals. He roamed the theater shooting our
act as we played, as well as the audience, and that stream was fed to one
of the monitors onstage too.

March 2, 1974. The room was well filled, though a lot of the crowd
was invited. We were all nervous. There was a tiny room off to the side
of the stage where we waited to go on. I had a couple of drinks. In those

days especially, my performances took place in a puppet realm, where everything I did originated in electrical nerves from which I dangled and projected. My behavior was a combination of extreme deliberation and complete loss of control. I liked to obliterate myself with the volume and relinquish myself, devote myself into the stage lights, as if they gave me privacy. My relationship was with the physics of the situation—the spotlight into which I aimed myself and my feelings, and the billowing skitters of sound pouring forward from behind me. I constantly felt this mix of consciousness that I was doing things wrong but that I also knew and employed a magic that transformed the mistakes as they happened into glory and stick-figure beauty and power, and that is what happened.

I was glad about the set we played. It worked; we were stunning, if rackety. I knew that everyone in the audience had gotten way more than their money's worth. Then I saw Tom's face when we were back offstage, and for a minute I really didn't understand. Then he said something, and I hated him. He was going to treat the show as an embarrassment, as humiliation. As nothing but an indication of how far short we were of what we should be. To him we were all just more-or-lessworkable pieces of equipment in his shop, or livestock to manipulate.

My stomach fell away. But the anger couldn't be expressed, I knew from experience, because that would be self-defeating. I had to retain belief that as the band gained experience, and audience reaction, we could return to the track that we'd shared at the beginning. I had to believe that this present tension was a detour. I could see our pure existence, and that all it would take would be a little bit of mutual respect and a sense of revelry in our being this band. I still held on to the hope that he could reawaken to the larger possibilities. I didn't really have any choice—I'd invested too much of myself in our prospects. So I gritted my teeth and continued.

It's true that the band sounded ragged. But this was something that had also been said of the early gigs (and often the later ones) of the New York Dolls and the Stooges and the Velvet Underground. It was something that I positively liked in a band. It's true of the Stones' *Exile on Main Street* sessions too, or on some of their early singles, like "Who's Driving Your Plane?" or "19th Nervous Breakdown." Another band whose sound I'd always loved was Smokey Robinson and the Miracles, especially on a track like "Going to a Go-Go," which sounds like it was recorded in an alley, the band banging on cardboard boxes and garbage cans. I love a racket. I love it when it seems like a group is slipping in and out of phase, when something lags and then slides into a pocket, like hitting the number on a roulette wheel, a clatter, like the sound of the Johnny Burnette trio, like galloping horses' hooves. It's like a baby learning how to walk, or a little bird just barely avoiding a crash to the dirt, or two kids losing their virginity. It's awkward but it's riveting, and uplifting and funny. In a way it's the aural representation of that feeling that makes the first time people feel the possibilities of rock and roll music in themselves the benchmark of hope and freedom and euphoria.

But that's not what Tom was interested in anymore. He heard these crystal-clear crisp sweet-guitar suites of highly arranged series of time and dynamics sections in his head, and they were about specific parts constructed for effects where everything was subordinate to what his guitar would be doing. It was all about his composing and playing, rather than any other value of the material or band.

CHAPTER SIXTEEN

———————————————————————

P eople talk about how bad-off the U.S. was economically in those years of the seventies and how filthy and crime-ridden New York was. It's true, but my friends and I in the East Village didn't know any better, and terms like "recession" and "stock market" were meaningless to us. The streets of the city were smelly with both garbage—sanitation workers were striking—and dog shit (the scoop law wasn't passed until 1978). On the Lower East Side, people assumed their apartments would be burglarized every two or three years. Many buildings and sometimes whole blocks in the area were burned out and abandoned, others staked by squatters. Drug-dealing gangs ruled districts. Sidewalks for blocks would be matted with blankets of housewares and junk peddled by the jobless. It was a slum, but it was where we wanted to live because it was cheaper than anywhere else while also hosting the best bookstores and movies and drugs and people and music.

Our band had to figure out where to play next. I'd noticed how the Dolls had associated themselves with a particular venue. If a band always played the same nights at the same place, it was easier for them to build a following, since anyone interested would always know where to find them. There were plenty of nasty, hungry little joints around.

We looked for a likely room. The bar owner would have nothing to lose, we figured to explain to him. If he let us play there every weekend for what we charged at the door, he'd get his bar take boosted by our crowd, and we'd be fine with letting in any of his regulars for free.

The way I remember it is that Verlaine and Lloyd were walking back from a rehearsal when they spotted CBGB on the Bowery, and then I went over there to look at it with them, and then we came back with Ork to make our proposition to the owner. Hilly Kristal had bought the bar only two months before. He always said it all began when Tom and I caught him outside painting the awning and told him we wanted to talk to him. Lloyd says it was him and Verlaine. There's also the tale that we built the stage. I don't remember that either, and it sounds like something Lloyd might make up.

The place already had that stubby white awning and the ugly stucco-style whipped white surface on its narrow street-front. The Bowery was, of course, literally synonymous with drunkenness and dereliction, and, only four months before we debuted there, CBGB had been the Palace Bar, adjunct drink dump to the Palace Hotel flophouse next door. The dark booze cave, renamed, retained its resigned, rejected Bowery clientele for quite a while after we arrived. It was also a favorite hangout for the Third Street Hells Angels club.

The venue had opened under Hilly's management in December '73. He'd always intended to have live music, and two or three odd acts had appeared in the months before we played there on March 31, 1974, the first of our initial venue-establishing series of consecutive Sundays at CBGB.

The poster I made for that first club date had two vertical columns side by side, the one on the left a set of four photos like a film strip: the top one showing us playing pool in CBGB's back room, and the three others frames of shivering vagrants—the group—huddled outside of it at night. I typed some words I wrote for the purpose in the column on the right:

Horses gallop in from all
sides rising in the air
as they converge. The guy
in the torn blue suit is
whispering Please kill me.
Verlaine rolls out of bed
rubbing his eyes for the
third time in two hours.
The bleach-blond takes
another pill and smiles
sweetly. Billy flicks on
the TV. The galloping
horses meet in the air.
Tears are streaming down . . .
Television appears through
the horses. No injuries
except the screen has
developed leaks where the
boys put their cigarets
out.

      A distant sound of
almost human laughter can
be heard as the characters
grow new lungs after
dozing off during their
successful attempt to
swim the channels.

Tom and I collaborated on the official band biographies we ran off as a press handout:

TOM VERLAINE—guitar, vocals, music, lyrics: Facts unknown.
RICHARD HELL—bass, vocals, lyrics: Chip on shoulder. Mama's boy. No personality. Highschool dropout. Mean.
RICHARD LLOYD—guitar, vocals: bleach-blond—mental institutions—male prostitute suicide attempts.
BILLY FICCA—drums: Blues bands in Philadelphia. Doesn't talk much. Friendly.

TELEVISION'S music fulfills the adolescent desire to fuck the girl you never met because you've just been run over by a car. Three minute songs of passion performed by four boys who make James

The pathology prevails.

Dean look like Little Nemo. Their sound is made distinctive by Hell's rare Dan Electro bass, one that pops and grunts like no model presently available, and his unique spare patterns. Add to this Richard Lloyd's blitzcrieg chop on his vintage Telecaster and Verlaine's leads alternately psychotic Duane Eddy and Segovia on a ukelele with two strings gone. Verlaine, who uses an old Fender Jazzmaster, when asked about the music said, "I don't know. It tells the story. Like 'The Hunch' by the Robert Charles Quintet or 'Tornado' by Dale Hawkins. Those cats could track it down. I'll tell you the secret."

I can't remember why I wrote, at the time it took place, the following account of one of the Sundays in those first three months. Presumably it was intended for one of the rock magazines whose editors I was then meeting, but it wasn't published at the time.

My First Television Set
"Jest the facts"—(Sgt. Friday) T. Verlaine ("Prove It")

I walked into this Bowery dive called C.B.G.B. on a Sunday night in April. The first thing I noticed was that it smelled liked dogshit. Then I saw the damned dog. Three or four girls were dancing and being totally ignored by the handsome young gents at the bar. "Talk Talk" by the Music Machine was playing loudly enough on the jukebox to preserve your privacy. A few people stood around the coin slot pool table in back and another thirty or forty sat at tables drinking. The place had a grapevine reputation on account of a band called Television that played there Sundays at midnight. It was a quarter after twelve.

The jukebox got turned off and four guys filed out, one stepping back up behind the drums on the little stage and the other three kneeling down in front of their amps to tune up. They were all skinny and had hair as short and dirty and ragged as their shirts. Their pants didn't fit very well but were pretty tight with the exception of one guy who was actually wearing a very baggy 20-year-old suit over his torn shirt. While the lights were still down they continued to tune for five minutes looking intense and sharing a cigarette. The pool table had got abandoned and some fancy looking numbers at the door were trying to talk their way past the $2.00 admission. A little guy with big shoulders in a Hawaiian shirt went over and told them to go back to New Jersey.

Finally one of the boys in the band stepped off behind the bar for a second and switched on the stage lights. When he got back he slipped on his guitar, eyed the audience and told us the name of the first song. The bass player banged off a figure and they broke into "Hard On Love."

I'll take them from right to left. The singer, Tom Verlaine, tall, blonde, and with a face like the Mr. America of skulls, stood at a slight angle from the mike with his eyes half closed and his black guitar strapped up high. He looked totally concentrated, his mouth moving with the slightest exaggeration as if it were the mechanical means, like a plane for seeding clouds, that enabled some terrific natural force to be released. But then when there was a solo or a few moments between words his whole body would slide backwards or droop to the side synchronized with a chord and then jerk in another direction, eyes shut like someone barely able to maintain consciousness. Rising back to the microphone just in time.

In the middle the other guitar player, Richard Lloyd, swiveled his head, holding his guitar low below his hips, bending over, his neck bulging, guitar nearly touching the floor as his feet went to cover every inch of the square yard allotted to them. A perfect male whore pretty boy face alive with such fear and determination as he wracked the guitar you could almost hear his mother scolding him. He looked like he was going to cry.

On the other side of him stood Richard Hell, the bass player, in black boots, the baggy suit, and sunglasses. Dark hair short on the sides but sticking out three inches from the top like anticipating the electric chair. He'd stand there head lolling off on his shoulder while he fingered the bass until a little drool rolled out of the side of his mouth and then suddenly make some sort of connection and his feet would start James Browning and he'd jump up in the air half splits and land hopping around utterly nuts with his lips pointed straight at you.

Billy Ficca on drums, meanwhile, up above and behind, was slamming and kicking in surprise beats, serious face listening and listening with eyes glazed. He was completely on top. His head held like you tilt your head to tune in on a sound, then moving it again a little, catching a cue, while his arms worked like mad always throwing in something to keep it moving while his eyes gazed off.

The sound of the music was just as raw, perverse and real as the band members looked. Bass like a dinosaur plucked with a claw while one guitar made shiny loops for the other to use at raygun practice. Then it would start raining on the ocean. You'd see a cymbal crash. A verse sung like the genuine sneer at stupid girls of an eight year old who then goes home and cries in his pillow. The three boys in front would step to their mikes and sing Hard on *love* Hard on *love*, then the singer solo: *Why* you gotta be so hard on love?? Four beat silence, drums kick it off and another verse starts up. All over in three and a half minutes. They looked so vulnerable and so cold at the same time I wondered how they'd lived long enough to get here.

Their lyrics were also a lot of things at once. Full of little designs. Sometimes funny or dirty or romantic, often psychotic. Some lines: "We'll steer by the stars in our high heeled cars" (High Heel Wheels), "My horse run away, my hennypennies don't lay and my cock just don't git up no more" (Bluebird), "Love comes in spurts for sure. Though sometimes it hurts far more, you just get love in spurts" ("Love In Spurts"), "Enfant Terrible. So many personae. You're so death-loose. That's not talking. Talking?" ("Enfant Terrible").

After a number people would clap and whistle, a few would yell Yay Television, the singer would thank them, and whoever was to sing the next number introduced it with a few words and they'd do something different. They played two forty-five minute sets, thanked everybody, and announced they'd be back the following Sunday. Me and some other people think they're the best band in the world. Anyway, I went home, started to write a book, and then asked my sister for a blow job.

Maybe that article says as much about my mind-set at the time as it does about the group, but those things were inseparable then. (If it had been published I, as writer, of course, would have used another assumed name; I wanted to enjoy setting a precedent for how the group should be viewed.)

"Hard on Love" was a lyric Verlaine had written to try to match "Love Comes in Spurts." "Foxhole" was another attempt at catch-up double entendre. It's ironic, because he always believed that other people were getting rich off his ideas. He had that closed-off self-obsessed paranoia and misconception of ownership. As a lyricist though, Tom was the king of his specialty—the mental "one hand clapping" line like "I fell into the arms of Venus de Milo" or "the lightning struck itself" or "a boat made out of ocean."

We immediately got attention and every week there'd be new notable people in the crowd at CBGB, but what we were doing only made sense to the sophisticated nightclubbers, the savvy New York music-business ones like Danny Fields—who'd managed the Stooges and was connected to the Max's Warhol crew—and his flitty journalist friends such as Lisa Robinson, or else alert musicians, like David Bowie and Bryan Ferry and Iggy Pop, or the young artists from the artists' bars and bookstores, and smart band-loving topless-dancing girls. At the time, to that pop artistic demimonde of connoisseurs, Television at CBGB represented the Future, the new turn the world was taking.

I'd been working with Patti Smith on preparing her book for publication with my Dot Books, so she and Lenny Kaye came to see Television early that spring and that was a turning point for both her and our band. Patti was the underground girl of the year in 1974, as Edie Sedgwick had once been, and Bette Midler after that, and Madonna later. When Patti saw us she realized she had company. She saw that we were as fresh and good in our area as she was in hers and it was time for her to connect to us and move more fully into music. She found a piano player to add to Kaye's guitar. She wrote an ecstatic account of Television for the new local weekly, the *SoHo News*, and she set her sights on Verlaine. For a few months they were a couple. She was also living with her boyfriend Allen Lanier of the Blue Öyster Cult at the time.

Patti's affair with Verlaine clinched the conflict between Tom and me. Inevitably, as his new girlfriend, she supported Tom in his differences with me, and at least tacitly accepted his denigration of me. She'd still wink and grin at me and act friendly and admiring and want to do this and that, but that didn't touch what she'd do with and for Tom, and any social or public reference to me by her became an empty formality in the context of her promotion of Verlaine. He became truly insufferable.

I had my partisans—the most significant, in retrospect anyway, being Malcolm McLaren. But at that time Malcolm's name didn't carry a lot of weight—and even if it had, it wouldn't have changed the widening split between Tom and me. It just meant I felt a little less betrayed and undervalued.

Malcolm was a young British clothing designer and boutique owner who was interested in the possibilities of rock and roll for affecting the culture. He was an artist and an intellectual. I probably wouldn't have described him exactly that way at the time, but most of it was apparent on some level. He was in and out of New York in 1974 and early 1975 in his role as last-ditch manager of the Dolls. They'd lost ground since the first wave of excitement about them. Their second album hadn't done as well as their first and their first hadn't been a hit either. It seemed like they might be too radical and sloppy and crude to move beyond New York. And, even among their own crowd, they'd lost ground to the CBGB's bands. Malcolm's main contribution to the Dolls was to dress them all in tight red leather and use a gigantic hammer-and-sickle Russian Communist flag as a backdrop for their shows. So they were not only fags but Commies. I was deeply impressed, but not many other people were. I mean it was obvious the guy'd misread American psychology, but it was a fantastic gesture anyway, like a perfect suicide note or famous last words. The Dolls went down defiant, and leaving a good-looking corpse.

Malcolm saw that Television represented an authentic shift in purpose and style, and the part that interested him was what I brought. The Dolls had been a culmination of hippie communal values, of classic blues-based rock and roll, of quasi-effeminate glam, while Television was the beginning of the rejection of hippie values and the rejection of star worship (even ironically), replaced by a furious, if icy at times— and somewhat poetic—alienation and disgust and anger, expressed in the way we looked and behaved, and in songs like "(I Belong to the) Blank Generation" and "Love Comes in Spurts" (as opposed to "All You Need Is Love"). He understood the conflict between Verlaine and me and he had no interest in Verlaine's position. He told me that if I left the band he'd do anything he could to help me. I appreciated that, but I knew I didn't want anyone looking over my shoulder. Malcolm was obviously a strong personality and I wanted to be on my own.

I performed publicly with Television at CBGB for a year, from the spring of 1974 through the spring of 1975. Five months after our debut, the Ramones, as we had, played at CBGB for the first club gig of their existence after financing their own earlier ones (in their case, at a rehearsal studio) and immediately became regulars. They were great. Tom sneered at them. The Stilettos, which was the early "girl group" incarnation of Blondie, also showed up for steady gigs. They were a harmonizing street-girl relative of the glittery, campy Dolls style, with Chris Stein writing music and playing guitar, and Debbie Harry one of the trio of girls who provided the vocals. Before that first year was out, Blondie and also the Patti Smith Group formed and debuted at CBGB, becoming regular headliners. The Talking Heads showed up just a shade after a year had passed, and the Dead Boys a year or so after that. Patti drew the biggest crowds. She was the most accomplished, talented sheer performer, though her band was generic and undistinguished, and her songs became more and more ordinary too. Television was also quite popular and was the most interesting band both musically and historically, if a bit inconsistent and esoteric. We were for the connoisseurs. The Ramones were popular but were regarded by the core movers as intrinsically minor, a kind of novelty act. They were a cool idea and one that was on the mark for the time, injecting subversive, funny real-life subject matter into roaring bubble gum, like the Stooges on surfboards, but, basically, a joke ("Beat On the Brat") and a formula. Hardly anyone took Blondie seriously. They had a bland, occasionally quirky, urban girl-group style but were primarily an excuse to look at their stunningly pretty singer. She had a flair for campy stylish thrift-store clothes and a street-smart, real-life, low-key, deep likability, but there wasn't anything new about the group. Of course, it was Blondie and the Ramones who ended up being the biggest popular successes.

more or less lived at the club, and at Max's Kansas City, for all of that first year, and the next two as well. CBGB was isolated. It had received virtually no national publicity, and even in New York it was a "downtown" phenomenon, known only to a minuscule subculture, though we fully expected to become international hits. The room was usually no more than half full even on weekends, and the larger crowds for even the most popular bands were conscious of their status as enlightened initiates. Most media people and their audiences didn't take rock and roll seriously. Even the veteran trash journalist Lisa Robinson, who was practically the only national voice to consistently play up the scene, with her magazines *Rock Scene* and *Hit Parader*, treated the movement as primarily a source of titillation and gossip, just another instance of decadent fashionable New York nightlife. Only a few of the musicians and their friends knew that what was going on at CBGB was the most interesting thing happening in the world at that time for both high art and popular culture.

The most important aspect of the isolation, though, was the way in which what happened within it was a dream come true, was a comprehensive self-invention, or self-manifestation. In retrospect, it seems like everything we did has been colored by the way the music has come to be perceived now, but that's not the way things really were—"punk" is too limited a description for what happened there from 1974 through 1977. On one hand the place was more mundane and half-assed than it's typically pictured as having been. There were plenty of ordinary derivative bands that could have been found anywhere at the time. But on the other hand we had conjured into existence, out of imagination, this reality in which we were the representatives, the sound and appearance and behavior, of the environment we'd located at CBGB. This was the essence of CBGB then and there—that we, with our rejected and extreme sets of beliefs and values and intentions, had managed to materialize an environment in which we were not outside, but at home ourselves. Where we were the positive standards of being, rather than examples of failure, depravity, criminality, and ugliness. It was a world of rock and roll and poetry and anger and revelry and drunkenness and sex, but all specific. It brought real life, as opposed to the conventions of popular songs, back to rock and roll, but starting from the real life of a very specific time and place. The traits and signs of what came to be called punk were the ways that we'd systematically invented or discovered as means for displaying on the outside what was inside us. That's the origin of the funny, lyrical, angry music styles, the haircuts, the clothes, the names, and everything else that identified us. What defined the club was that it was where we were completely ourselves. And what could be better than that?

I had two girlfriends for more than a night or two that year. One was Roberta Bayley. I met her two weeks after Television's first date at CBGB, at a New York Dolls gig at Club 82, a dark sub-street-level room that was the perfect environment for the Dolls, having been a tight-knit little mob-owned drag club for decades. It was downstairs on East Fourth Street between Second and Third Avenues. That show was the only time in the Dolls' career that they actually played in full drag (all except macho Italian Johnny, who refused to come out in a skirt, though he wore plenty of makeup and quite high heels). David Johansen wore a glittering strapless cocktail dress. The group was in top form and the place was packed, the crowd a roiling flood below the stage, faces like the flower cargo of a wrecked ship strewn across the waves. You couldn't help but get slap-happy in it as you were washed around and the band joked and busted out in muscular girliness and blaring drums and guitars in the glare.

Roberta was very pretty and I was sure I'd see her again. You could tell she appreciated an up-to-date young musician, but she was self-possessed and smart. She'd just arrived in town from London, to which she'd escaped after dropping out of college in San Francisco.

I was at the club all night that night without quite realizing it. When I finally climbed the stairs and pushed open the door to the sidewalk, alone, I was surprised by the dawn. Everything was quiet, the gray-blue air still, and just there, a few yards ahead, was Johnny Thunders ducking into a taxi by himself. It was thrilling and inspiring. He was Johnny Thunders of the Dolls offstage, alone. Taking a taxi. I could never take taxis because they cost too much.

Roberta would end up playing a big role in our new world as a photographer, even though she'd never taken a picture before. (In fact the very first band pictures she took were of the Heartbreakers a year and a half later, when I was in the group with Thunders. Those were the black and white shots, one of which was eventually used on the cover of Legs McNeil's and Gillian McCain's punk oral history *Please Kill Me*, for which I'd spattered our shirtfronts with chocolate syrup as blood—à la black and white Hollywood movies—to illustrate my slogan for a gig poster, "Catch them while they're still alive.") Roberta handled the door at CBGB at the beginning, originally for Television, selling tickets ($2) and deciding who got in free. She became the main

Roberta Bayley at her post, CBGB.

staff photographer for John Holmstrom's groundbreaking *Punk* magazine once it started up in 1976. When we met, though, she had no
credentials except for being a rock and roll lover of refined sensibilities.
She was a party girl without being promiscuous. Celebrity didn't im-
press her. Everybody liked her. We ended up going together for two or
three months, and she stayed my friend. She had the prettiest breasts
I'd ever seen. But most importantly, she was kind and had heart. She
stuck by me through everything.

The other girl from that year I saw steadily for a while was Elda Gen-
tile, one of the singers in the Stilettos. She *was* a slut (like me) and that
was great too. Elda came out of the hardass but sweet, adventurous,
fringe-Warhol Max's scene. She had a baby kid, Branch, whose father

was Eric Emerson, the classically pretty blond Factory regular who'd been in a few Warhol movies and had started a glam band called the Magic Tramps. Elda was funny. She used to give me advice, recognizing me as the next wave.

It was interesting how playing rock and roll made a person handsome. I hadn't been handsome before. My looks improved partly because I kind of knew what I was doing, that I was using the shift into music life to re-create myself. But it was also rock and roll itself. It made a person handsome.

The women at CBGB were interesting too. There were intellectual high school girls and band-happy go-go dancers, pretty photographers, girl journalists, and slumming rich nightclubbing types, not to mention women band members. The topless dancers probably predominated, at least in my consciousness, but the categories overlapped. Some of the topless dancers were also intellectual teenagers who wrote about bands and came from uptown (which pretty well describes Kathy Acker, come to think of it). Most just liked to get high and spend their nights with young musicians. I liked almost all of them.

Being a rock and roll musician was like being a pimp. It was about making young girls want to pay money to be near you. That was the relationship with the anonymous audience, and the audience you actually met as well. I was always ready to fall in love, but I had noticed that love comes in spurts, and that was appreciated by the women. Many of them expected or even required that their boyfriends neglect them a little—it proved how important the boyfriends were. (Of course, most of the dancers came from unhappy family backgrounds; relationships were expected to include abuse.)

The go-go dancers made a lot more money than the band members did, and they shared it freely. One of the most powerful mental images

I retain from those days involves a girlfriend from a few months later, in 1975, after I'd left Television and had started in with the Heartbreakers. Her name was Carol and she was a nineteen-year-old topless dancer from rural Pennsylvania. She had long straight natural blond hair and the face of a confused cheerleader. Her body was like a compilation of American male fantasies: so youthfully ripe that, while having no excess, it seemed to be straining to burst from itself, with breasts that lifted as if they were scenting the air, an athlete's high butt that sheltered under it that little concave-sided triangle of light between the tops of her thighs, behind the soft lush see-through-blond pubic hair; and she was uncomplicated and good-natured and desirous to please.

I was doing junk pretty often by then, but it still felt deluxe. I was sure that the drug was outlawed because the arrogant rich wanted it to themselves. Sticking a needle in my arm felt adult, like I was really in charge of myself finally, running my own destiny, out from under. It was more independent than any other choice I'd ever made.

Carol often had to work at night dancing in midtown, so she wasn't always able to catch second sets at the club. She gave me the keys to her apartment, and, after I was paid for a gig—maybe $50 on a good night—I'd likely go cop a couple of bags of dope and then let myself into her place to wait until she got off work at two or three AM.

One of those late nights, I was lying alone in semidarkness in her big bed in that continuous soft slo-mo rippling of dope bliss, dreaming and drifting, when she let herself in. The trebly crunch of the key in the door distracted me out of my nod. She saw me and broke into smiles and jumped up, in her miniskirt and tight blouse, onto the bed, bright-eyed, straddling my torso, standing, center panel of creased 3-D panties directly above my eyes, and reached into her pockets and purses to lift out fistfuls and fistfuls of soft crinkled money she released to float down all over me.

By the winter of 1974–75, Tom was shutting me out beyond a doubt. He had not only stopped allowing most of my songs onto set lists, but he'd told me not to move around onstage while he sang. He didn't want any attention distracted from himself. The last straw came when Virgin records asked for a demo recording of the band, to be produced by Brian Eno. Out of six songs to be recorded, Tom would play only one of mine, "Blank Generation," and he performed it like a novelty song.

In early 1975, Malcolm invited us to open for the Commie red-leather Dolls at the Little Hippodrome ballroom in midtown, in what would turn out to be the full Dolls' last New York show, on February 28, 1975. It was also one of my last appearances with Television. In late March, a week after I quit the band, I got a call at Cinemabilia from Johnny Thunders. He said that he and the Dolls' drummer, Jerry Nolan, had just left the band, and wanted to know if I would join them to sing, write songs, and play bass in a new group to be called the Heartbreakers.

didn't know Johnny that well. I'd had a few drinks with him, and he'd seen me in Television a few times, but I didn't know he was so into me that he'd ask me to make a band with him. I didn't hesitate. It increased my respect for him! I wanted to make tough, frantic music, and that's what Johnny did, and he was the most exciting guitar-playing stage presence of the time.

Jerry had named the Heartbreakers. It wasn't awful, and I didn't want to start the band with an argument. We did a photo session before we even had a rehearsal. We went over to the grungy, broke-down Hudson River waterfront and posed for some pimply, frayed, windblown pictures for mellow, goodhearted Bob Gruen, the Dolls' camp follower and house photographer. Johnny still had the ratty black stacked-up super-long hair that's imitated by every glam heavy-metal mug to this day. Nolan wore his natty Irish/Italian doo-wopper Queens street-style getup, which often included white or two-tone shoes and sharply creased form-fitting shirts and pants in bright colors. Somewhat Soupy Sales. I was a bit shaggier on top than usual—I wasn't careful about keeping my haircut in prime shape—and wore tight black jeans with some burn holes in them (left them too long to dry in the oven one night), scuffed jazz dance shoes, and a ragged suit jacket over my torn T-shirt.

pimply, frayed, windblown

Our rehearsals were casual. Gruen took more pictures at our first one, at the loft the Dolls kept on Twenty-Third Street. He shot us outside on the fire escape. Malcolm was there that afternoon too. He was a little worried about me. He was afraid that I might be wasting time with Johnny and Jerry, or, worse, that it could be dangerous to my health, that I'd end up as a junkie. I didn't really realize it at the time, but Johnny's and Jerry's drug use played a big part in their departure from the Dolls. They had chippies—rudimentary drug habits—closer to full-blown addiction than me. I thought they'd just gotten frustrated with the way things had slowed down for the Dolls and didn't like the disapproval of their drug proclivities from others in the group, but it was a little past that. Malcolm was not judgmental but he was down on narcotics. He took me aside and reminded me that I might be better off coming to London, where he would help me get a new start. I was happy about the Heartbreakers though, and I didn't want a controlling manager.

Johnny and Jerry had gotten used to a higher standard of living than me, but our careers were still pretty scroungy. We'd be lending each other a few bucks here and there. Everybody was free with what money there was, as poor people will be. It was another couple of months before I was able to quit Cinemabilia.

Through connections of Johnny's we got the use of a beat-up rehearsal loft in SoHo, where we practiced three or four days a week, and would usually cop a bag of dope each afterwards. There was speed around that year too and we'd use that sometimes. A friend of the band was Frenchy, another Dolls-entourage survivor, sometimes referred to as the Dolls' "valet." He was a dedicated speed freak. That whole Dolls gang was a ball of nonstop hedonism, though David and Syl were a bit more sober.

Life during most of the year I spent with the Heartbreakers was the best I would have in a band, in terms of good times. Dope was still nothing but fun, Johnny and Jerry were easygoing, and the group had a great sound and style. We were popular. I was the principal singer of the band, though Johnny sang four or five of his own songs. His songs, unambitious in ways, were often more powerful than mine. He and Jerry had already been playing them for a while, and not only had they jelled, but they were made to existing patterns, usually fifties and early sixties rock and roll, like Eddie Cochran or girl groups. I was still trying to teach myself how to write songs that would do what I wanted them to. But our sets were driving and rocking, and at their best they combined the different things that Johnny and I brought—my intellectual ambitions and lost-boy affect with Johnny's defiant junkie prowling. I got to live the ideal I'd had in mind when I came to New York to be a poet—to have a well-placed platform for saying things to the world, and an audience that thrived on it and wanted to have sex with me because of it, and I ran my own life, had no boss. And there were drugs and money.

One late afternoon hanging out with Roberta, sitting in a bar in midtown, I didn't feel like going to rehearsal so I got her to call the loft and say I couldn't make it because I'd been arrested. It worked perfectly; plausible, but partly for being too crazy to be made up, and anyway, Johnny and Jerry were usually fine with calling off a rehearsal.

I moved at this time, in early 1975, from Elizabeth Street to an apartment on Twelfth Street between First Avenue and Avenue A. I didn't move after that. The building was right on the border between the seedy youth area of the East Village, which still housed a lot of poor East European immigrants too, and the full-blown ghetto of deep Alphabet City, with its drugs and unromantic poverty. On Tenth Street and Avenue A, two blocks from me, in front of the abandoned corner storefront that had formerly housed the Psychedelicatessen, New York's first hippie head shop, milled a mob of twelve-to-fifteen-year-old heroin runners. I could walk around the corner and give a young teenager $3 and he'd be back in two minutes with a bag of dope. The story was that, as juveniles, they couldn't be sent to jail.

The junk trade was booming. Whole local blocks, in the course of a year or two, morphed from dwellings into darkness into drug hives. Hordes of junkies slipped money under hallway doors in abandoned buildings, and tiny taped-shut glassine envelopes were slid back. The dope's brand name would be rubber-stamped on the package, sometimes with a graphic logo, like "Toilet" or "Tombstone." The best brands would draw crowds of shoppers in lines that wound down tenement stairs and halfway up the burned-out block, in a single file kept orderly by the dealers' crew. Sometimes a scout would yell *"Bajando!"* and it would echo in relays around a few blocks and everyone would reluctantly disperse for a few minutes until the cops passed by.

Dee Dee would often come over to my apartment to visit and we would go around the corner and get ourselves each a bag of dope from the baby runners. Dee Dee was practically a baby himself, in his boy bob and his eagerness. It never occurred to me at the time, but I've read that Roberta says that Dee Dee secretly would have liked to be a Heartbreaker. This might have been true a couple or five years later, when he'd become a hard-core junkie. I can imagine him chafing at the regimented comic book style of the Ramones and wishing he could be in a real happy-go-lucky bad-boy band that attracted the more fun girls and wouldn't try to hamper his drug use. But back in 1975 he seemed happy in the Ramones; he was excited about them. At that time he didn't know any of the Heartbreakers but me.

Dee Dee, like Johnny and Jerry, and Richard Lloyd, and Gruen, never much cared about the quantity of factual content in the stories he told. He was probably the most uninhibited fabricator of punk anecdotes of them all, especially since he eventually published a lot of "autobiography" and gave a lot of interviews and was such a comic riot. He was like a boy Marilyn Monroe or Jessica Simpson with his cute dizzy-dumb persona. In rock and roll, in show business, there's not much value placed on integrity. People say and do what serves their interests and what seems entertaining. That's just as well, if for no other reason than that it's inevitable. Ultimately what difference does it make what actually happened? Things look different from different perspectives, and the conquerors write history; and what reality do the stories of the past have except as entertainment and mythology? Obviously, "reality" is slippery anyway. "Print the legend," as advised in *The Man Who Shot Liberty Valance.*

Still, to me, it's interesting to try to figure out what's actually going on, what really happened. I want to get the most accurate idea I can of the way things are. To me, that's a lot of what "art" is about. Of course I have my vested interests too: even disregarding any pride involved, my earning power depends partly on my reputation and my role in past events, so I might try to straighten the record where I regard it as misrepresenting me. But I try to be as faithful to what happened as I can, however what happened might reflect on me. I want that to be part of my reputation too. Whereas Dee Dee's purposes were served more by keeping it funny, and maybe "funny" is more real than "true."

I always liked seeing Dee Dee, and to my mind he was the best example of a certain rock and roll essence that punk sought to embody. He was a street kid who was purely talented—he wrote most of the great Ramones songs—and who radiated lovable innocence, even though he'd worked, for lack of any better way to earn a living, as a gay hustler on the street. Or maybe that's where he'd learned the innocence. Like Jerry Nolan, he'd been a hairdresser for a while, too. He had a strongly defined personality—that funny dizzy dumb style—that he had to have developed as a defense. He was like a toddler, stumbling and misunderstanding what just happened, but who recovers instantly to plow ahead grinning proudly, endearingly, hilariously. With him the comedy was deliberate, if so deeply habitual that it became who he was. The other side of his childlike goofiness was his tantrums. But he

I always liked seeing Dee Dee

was so funny, usually about himself. My favorite example is something he said for a piece I did about the Ramones for *Hit Parader* in 1976. (It was the first time I'd done any journalism and the first article about the Ramones in a national publication.)

The band had gathered at Arturo Vega's loft for the interview. Arturo was the Ramones' art director and best friend and main booster. I turned on the tape recorder and started asking questions. In a minute, Dee Dee was explaining the group's songs and he said the first one they'd written was "I Don't Wanna Walk Around with You," and the next one was "I Don't Wanna Get Involved with You," and then "I Don't Wanna Go Down to the Basement." I don't wanna this and I don't wanna that. Finally he offered, "We didn't write a positive song until 'Now I Want to Sniff Some Glue.'" Someone who was actually dumb would never be able to think of that, which of course makes it even funnier.

Dee Dee is the best punk example of a rock and roll star in part because of that combination of his talent and his personal style, but especially because it's hard to imagine that he could have succeeded at anything else. The Sex Pistols famously screamed, "No future!" at the end of "God Save the Queen." People made a big deal about how progressive it was that a hit band could sarcastically rage about social conditions. But the noteworthy thing to me about the "no future" subject isn't the Sex Pistols' anger about their boring prospects as citizens, but rather that the lack of a future is an unacknowledged foundation of rock and roll. There is no future in being an adolescent, and rock and roll is the music of adolescence.

Rock and roll is the only art form at which teenagers are not only capable of excelling but that actually requires that one be a teenager, more or less, to practice it at all. This is the way that "punk" uniquely embodies rock and roll. It explicitly asserts and demonstrates that the music is not about virtuosity. Rock and roll is about natural grace, about style and instinct. Also the inherent physical beauty of youth. You don't have to play guitar well or, by any conventional standard, sing well to make great rock and roll; you just have to have it, have to be able to recognize it, have to *get it.* And half of that is about simply being young, meaning full of crazed sex drive and sensitivity to the object of romantic and sexual desire, and full of anger about being condescended to by adults, and disgust and anger about all the lies you're being fed, and all the control you've been subjected to, by those complacent adults. And a deep desire for some fun. And, though rock and roll is about being cool, you don't have to be cool to make real rock and roll—sometimes the most innocuous and pathetic fumblers only become graced by the way they shine in songs. And this is half of what makes the music the art of adolescence—that it doesn't require any verifiable skill. It's all essence, and it's available to those who, to all appearances, have nothing.

I'd seen a picture or two of Sabel Starr in magazines like *Creem* that covered the Dolls. She and Thunders were the sensational love duo of that ghetto of rock and roll fandom for a few months in 1972–73, and there was a lot of gossip and backstage/nightclub snapshots of them. Sabel was fifteen (Johnny was nineteen) when they met and she was already notorious as an L.A. groupie. Word was she'd slept with Iggy Pop when she was thirteen. In between Iggy and Johnny she'd been with Robert Plant, and in between Johnny and me she spent some time with Keith Richards. She and I got together in 1975.

Like the other avant-garde underage groupies of L.A., she dressed in an elaborate thrift-store old-school-movie-star/hooker style, with plenty of satin and silk, and fishnet stockings and Hollywood hats, sometimes with veils, and fake fur and spike heels and hot pants and feather boas. She looked like a pubescent trailer-camp drug whore, except that because we had no concept of a drug whore at that point, it might be more appropriate to say she looked like a flamboyant dress-up Lolita, especially since she always had the cheeriest healthy smile. The smile was real—happy and friendly. Everything about her was real. She was heroic. At least from the point of view of a musician whom she liked. She truly lived for fun and joy, and the thing that was the most joyous of all to her was to make a meaningful rock musician happy. That was her mission, the way someone else might join the Peace Corps. Instead of digging wells and planting crops and offering medical care, she provided pretty and entertaining companionship, astute and sincere encouragement, favorite drugs, and magnificent blow jobs.

She and Johnny had been broken up for a while when Johnny introduced me to her, and she and I spent a lot of time together in the following few months. She said just about the nicest thing that anyone had ever said to me. She told me that, at any time in the future, for the rest of my life, if I had the desire, all I had to do was ask her and she'd suck my cock. (One other person has said this to me and that was Rene Ricard, the poet and art writer. The difference is that we'd never had sex, and I would expect that, in fact, his offer expired, at the latest, once I gained fifteen pounds or my face got lined. But I think Sabel really meant it.)

She was a soulful, sane, self-aware sweetheart of a committed groupie. Cynics and some feminists mock the idea of the prostitute with a heart of gold. Groupies in Sabel's class are not prostitutes—on the contrary, they are humanitarian benefactors. But some groupies were part-time or occasional prostitutes who did also have hearts of gold, as do a meaningful number of nongroupie women who make their living from exercising their sex appeal in various ways, including escorting a person to orgasm. Of course some groupies were psycho fiends—the Nancy Spungen type.

I went out with Nancy for a while too, for a month or two in the year before she went to England and found Sid. I didn't know Sid very well—we only talked two or three times—but I liked him, and I got a strong feeling of who he was. Dee Dee was literally a role model for Sid—Sid's favorite rock stars were Johnny Thunders and Dee Dee—and he and Dee Dee had a lot in common. I knew Connie, Dee Dee's psycho-whore girlfriend who stabbed him in the butt (she had also knife-cut Arthur Kane of the Dolls when she was going out with him), though I never hung out with her. Among the pairings of musicians

With Sabel Starr.

with that species of girlfriend, I liked being with the men, I didn't like being with the women. The women were evidence of the insecurities and the low self-respect of the men. The men had problems, but at least they were self-aware and amusing. Most of them had a lot of charm, and a couple of them had a lot of talent. The women were egomaniacal, deluded manipulators, preying on the men (though Courtney did lead a great band). Granted, the men were in bad enough shape that they couldn't do much better for companionship.

Sid understood that he was a comedy of helplessness and uselessness. That doesn't mean he could have been any less a stumblebum, but just that he was self-aware, and because of that he was twice as funny and sympathetic. He could be violent too, but it was the violence of bewilderment and self-destruction and opportunism. He wasn't really vicious. He just saw that there was a crazy opening into fame and money that required only that he relax into full loutish negativity.

There were two things about Nancy, apart from her insanity, that were different from the other sex-worker girls who liked the bands at CBGB—she regarded herself as smarter than the rest of the girls, and she was exceedingly driven to rise in the world of rock and roll, in the hierarchy of it, and the only means she had was as a girlfriend.

We went out for maybe six weeks, towards the end of my time in the Heartbreakers, around late 1975. She still dressed in clothes you could find at Macy's—low-budget office and schoolgirl togs—though that included fetish boots, and she used a lot of eye makeup and bright lipstick. She was like a slutty suburban girl cruising the mall. She lived in a small studio apartment on West Twenty-Third Street, where she had a Bad Company poster on the wall. When something impeded her in her groupie-vocational mission, you could actually see in her eyes how all of an avid sudden the wheels started spinning in her head. It was a dazed look and the tone of her voice broke as she groped to right things. You would realize that as flatteringly desirous of your company and as eager to please you as she was, it was impersonal, because she was so fully programmed. There wasn't any connection between the pair of you.

When I had had enough of spending time with her and told her I didn't want to get together anymore, she was instantly possessed by naked, shameless disappointment and she started crying and begging me to give her another chance. She pleaded that she'd do anything, and she turned around and pulled her panties down and leaned up against the wall to demonstrate it.

To be fair, that's not all that creepy. Another girl I went out with for a long time, many years later, and really cared about and respected, did something similar when we were separating. She took Polaroids of herself naked in certain positions and gave them to me, telling me that I could do whatever I wanted with the real thing. The difference was that when that girlfriend did that it made me feel like a messed-up person, but when Nancy did it it made her seem like a messed-up person. I shouldn't say that about Nancy. I don't want to begrudge her her moment (the one with Sid, not the one with me). Again, it's part of the beauty of rock and roll that it's about people with no conventional skill, but only assertive youthfulness, becoming fascinating.

Who's good and who's bad anyway? People like the villains as often as they like the heroes. Americans love winners all the more if they lied and cheated and coerced to get to the top. People admire mobsters like Joe Gallo or John Gotti—or con men like P. T. Barnum or Colonel Tom Parker, or ruthless tycoons like Jeff Bezos or Joe Kennedy. Baseball, the apotheosis of romantic American self-image, is a good example of the national appreciation for winning dirty. Does a guy sliding into second ever honorably return to the dugout because he knows he was tagged before he touched base? No, the player cheats and lies if it increases his chance of winning. We take that for granted as built into the national pastime. Americans are not "gentlemen." Baseball is not cricket, which is played differently because the object is not "to win" but to get exercise, and the players are "gentlemen." In America losers are considered fools if they haven't played dirty enough. Winning justifies everything.

---

met Lizzy Mercier when she first came to New York from Paris at the end of 1975, when I had just turned twenty-six and she was eighteen, nearly nineteen. On that trip she was only here for a week or two. She returned for a longer time in early 1976.

She was traveling with Michel Esteban, who was about my age. Esteban had a rock and roll clothing boutique in Paris. He and Lizzy had come to New York because they had heard about what the CBGB bands were doing. Michel and Lizzy were just about to start their magazine *Rock News*, which would be the first, apart from *Punk*, focused on the scene at CBGB, and, soon, the one in London.

I never knew in those first few months if Lizzy and Michel were having sex. I assumed they'd originally been lovers. I went through some emotional contortions regarding Lizzy's relationship with him, but ultimately I had to decide not to care what she did when she wasn't with me and to expect the same attitude from her. Our ways of life made exclusivity unrealistic. In another sense, for our first year or two, it could be hard to believe we were together even when we were in the same room. We literally couldn't understand each other, since she spoke very little English and I spoke no French. But we were crazy about each other.

I first saw her across the crowded room at CBGB on a night I was playing there with the Heartbreakers. When our eyes met it was like the sound in the room went off and pin spots lit us. She was wearing bright slippers and shiny skintight leather pants and a freshly laundered and ironed men's white dress shirt with cufflinks. She had the head of a feline tomboy, with hair so wild and abundant it looked like it would have leaves and twigs in it. Her hips were shapely if childishly slim and there was a defiant lift to her flat nose. She had plush lips and the most clear skin. She was a wraith but assertive. She came back with me to my apartment that night, but she was modest, unsure about how much sex was proper in those first few hours. She blushed.

Right away, it felt like we were uniquely linked, even if we half imagined ourselves into our relationship. Our life together was walled off from everything else in the world. In our conceptions of ourselves we were inseparable; we were lovers and the only family in the world, like Adam and Eve, if he were a seedy addict poet of a musician private eye, and she was an intellectual sex-kitten chanteuse adventuress little girl. But we both lived and trusted our imaginations. We'd realized them. That was the dreamiest dream of all. We had already made our dreams real.

I didn't believe in love. I believed in science, in chemistry. Lizzy and I had chemistry that was stronger than "love." I've heard that Plato theorized that men and women were originally one and that's why they are attracted to each other: to become whole again. Lizzy and I didn't need to know much more about each other than that we belonged together. It stayed that way for both of us for much of the rest of her life, though soon enough we rarely acted on it because actually being with each other was often hard work: we never were able to fit the reality to that particular dream well for extended peri-

it felt like we were uniquely linked

ods. The dream took place in instants, or in substrata. We were like fictional characters in that way too—once the romance is consummated the story is usually over.

Sophisticated people discreetly refrain from speculating about, much less judging, what goes on between couples. Every marriage is its own culture, and even within it, mystery is the environment. There's that story in *Citizen Kane* about a man once seeing an unknown girl going the other direction on a passing ferry and realizing she's the love of his life. (Welles had a million of them, stories and girls.) I don't actually think my life would have been much different if I'd never met Lizzy, whereas, for instance, even though I only spent two years with Patty Oldenburg, she and her sophisticated lightheartedness and her world of brilliant art hugely changed my life. My wife, Sheelagh, has had an incalculable impact on my life, by far the largest impact of any woman I've known. For years I thought of Lizzy as my soul mate, but I don't think anything would have been much different if we'd never met. We were dreams of each other. Twice we nearly got married, but when it came down to it I knew better at some level and canceled.

It's a perfect metaphor that we didn't speak the same language except in all signifiers but words. It also helped to keep us from ever lying to each other. I don't think we did ever lie to each other. And as over the years she became more and more fluent in English, we only became more friendly, and still we never did lie, though there were areas where we didn't trespass.

Lizzy was the inspiration for the love interest in my first novel, *Go Now* (1996), and my song "(I Could Live With You) (In) Another World" was addressed to her.

We were both species of minor hustler, hustlers of culture and of our characters and bodies, but we weren't cynical or hard-bitten. We were a kind of Hansel and Gretel of culture hustling. It's just that we wanted to live by our wits in the worlds of human-made beauty and pleasure rather than anything more regimented and secure.

Patti Smith was Lizzy's other great New York supporter and admirer in those early days. I wondered if they had sex, but I never knew, and it wasn't something that really concerned me, except that I didn't trust that Lizzy was anything but an ornament for Patti. I assumed Lizzy had sex with women at times just because she was friends with women who were obviously attracted to her and I doubted if Lizzy would be especially inhibited when occasions arose. But Patti was elsewhere when Lizzy was dying. Michel Esteban always seemed to me to

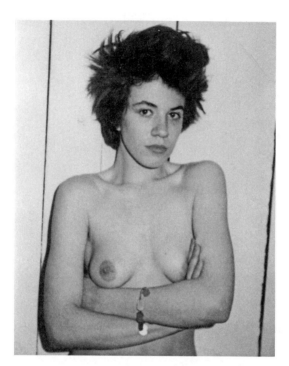

Lizzy was the inspiration

be playing up Patti's presence in Lizzy's history because he thought it was good for Lizzy's career.*

I remember how, once, in the first year I knew her, I visited Lizzy at the bare apartment she was using in New York, and I opened the refrigerator and it was completely empty except for a shelf on the door lined with colorful tiny jars of baby food—strained carrots and mashed peas and pureed plums. She'd seen the stuff in a market and bought some and discovered she liked it. She did hardly anything like other people.

---

* Within two or three years of Lizzy's first visit to New York she was making records. Michel had started a record company called ZE in partnership with a very rich young entrepreneur named Michael Zilkha (ZE = Zilkha Esteban). Both Michaels tended to take pretty, vivacious, smart, charismatic young women as protégées they'd attempt to make into recording stars. The label's genre specialty was noise ("no wave") and funk, often combined. Lizzy's records often had African music backing. She had a hit dance single ("Mais où sont passées les gazelles?") in France, recorded with black African musicians in South Africa, in 1984. I wasn't really conscious of her music career and I believe she took it pretty casually too. It was primarily another means of getting her to tropical seas around the world. I only ever saw her perform live once, at the nightclub of its moment, Nell's, on West Fourteenth Street in New York, sometime in the late eighties or early nineties. She didn't look comfortable there. But she always looked great on the album covers, and in fact I've discovered from YouTube that in the right environment, Lizzy was a knockout seller of a song, too, dancing so fine, in some of the African music videos and French TV she did.

CHAPTER TWENTY

B ob Quine, the violently sublime guitar player on most of my recordings, told me, a little while after I got to know him, that he'd been at the first Heartbreakers gig at CBGB in August 1975. He said I was chewing gum as I played and that at a certain moment in the performance I aggressively spat the wad some distance, and he said that that's when he knew I was a star. I remember that gig. We were doing speed in that period. Speed went well with punk. The Sex Pistols liked speed (sometimes mixed with acid).

It's true, the Heartbreakers were a good group. I first met Jake Riviera (original name: Andrew Jakeman), the British rock and roll hardass impresario of the pub-rock groups, in my early Heartbreakers days. He discovered and/or managed Elvis Costello and Nick Lowe and the Damned, and he cofounded Stiff Records, and, later, Radar Records. But when I met him he was still a blue-collar road manager for Dr. Feelgood. The road manager travels with the band, overseeing the logistics of touring—it's field labor, comparable to a work-gang foreman, as opposed to the manager proper, who is the mastermind overseer of a band's career. The Feelgoods were working-class English white guys who played super-fast, aggressive R & B. When they gigged in New York in 1975, Jake visited CBGB and saw the Heartbreakers and then waited to talk to me. He took me to dinner with Lee Bril-

the Heartbreakers were a good group

leaux, the lead singer of the Feelgoods, and some other people in their bunch, and told me that the Heartbreakers' set that night had been the best rock and roll show he'd ever seen, and he'd seen a lot of shows. He ended up standing behind his words by helping me out over and over in the coming years, and it all trickled down from that one set of the Heartbreakers.

Whenever I see any references to the Heartbreakers when I was in it, people are taking sides, favoring either Johnny or me, as if we were rivals and that to like one is to reject the other. That's wrong. I've always admired Johnny, and have never minded admitting it, and, after all, he approached me to ask me to join the band as singer and writer, not to mention bass player.

As I said about him in a memorial article the week of his funeral (in 1991), Johnny, contrary to his luggish image, was genuinely smart. That doesn't mean he read books or discussed issues and ideas. (Though towards the end of his life he did get political, writing songs about social issues and saying he supported Jesse Jackson for president.) He was smart in the same way that he dressed so perfectly. Smart the same way Elvis Presley was. You couldn't top him and he didn't delude himself. All charismatic people are smart, in the same sense that it's the fittest that survive—tautologically. But that doesn't make it any less valid. Stupid people look stupid; a charismatic person never looks stupid; therefore a charismatic person is smart. But the fact is that Thunders was positively smart. For instance, he noticed when a lyric I wrote was bad. One of my songs in the Heartbreakers was "Love Comes in Spurts." Its first two verses went:

I was a child
who wanted love that was wild
though tight as slow motion
but crazed with devotion

insane with devotion
from some other ocean
I was fourteen and a half
and it wasn't no laugh

and there was one line in those eight that bothered me. I always winced when it came to mind. Then one day Johnny kidded me about the lameness of "from some other ocean." He knew it was fake and overblown. You wouldn't think of him as a literary critic, but his perceptions were sharp.

Of course he was even lazier than me. He may not have ever written anything as corny as "from some other ocean," but his lyrics were half-assed in never having an original idea or turn of phrase. But good songs aren't about literary invention (though it's possible for them to have it, and I like trying).

Johnny did cultivate idiocy in his audiences (something the skinhead, soccer-thug element in English punk especially brought out in him), and he had a lot of idiot fans and they like to trash me. Nolan also actively fed that attitude after I left the band, when, from ruffled pride, he'd put me down in interviews. It was partly the Queens street-gang mentality that he and Thunders shared. I actually liked Jerry too, though I'd get pissed off when I saw some of the things he said, about how I couldn't make it as a poet so I'd moved to rock and roll, and how I was pretentious and egotistical. (Granted, there's truth there.) But the worst thing was the flat-out lie that I'd quit the Heartbreakers after trying somehow to get him, Nolan, to come over to my side from Johnny, to make me bandleader. Nothing remotely like that happened. I can't even conceive that situation. Johnny and Jerry were a unit, and I also accepted happily, was glad, that the Heartbreakers had no leader. (It was only sometime after I left the group that they began billing themselves as Johnny Thunders's Heartbreakers, partly to distinguish themselves from Tom Petty's band.)

My leaving the band was really about ambition level. For them the band was basically a party, or, when not, it was the ride to the party. I loved the way they played, and I loved Johnny's song-making instincts and rock and roll style altogether, and I liked the party, but I wanted the songs to talk about things other than "going steady" and "pirate love." I also wanted to try some new ways of playing. There was no way to bring this up with the Heartbreakers. If I was going to do those things it would have to be in a band with which I shared certain other aims and one that I led unequivocally. (Ironically, I realized that at this point I actually needed the same relationship with a band that Tom had gotten for himself by forcing me out of Television. We each ultimately needed a band we led.) So, in early 1976, I quit the Heart-breakers.

CHAPTER TWENTY-ONE

I first met Robert Quine when he started working at Cinemabilia in 1975. At that time he was pretty demoralized. Actually, he was permanently demoralized, but it was worse before he got the chance to publicly turn himself inside out and present the whole funny psycho-gore dissection as absolute music. Rock and roll guitar playing was the only endeavor he had any interest in practicing, but he had no reputation as a musician, was over thirty (b. December 30, 1942), was bald, and dressed in jeans and a sports jacket and a wrinkled button-down shirt, and there was no guitar-auditioning rock and roll band that didn't dismiss him on sight. (He never forgave people like Lenny Kaye who made the wrong kinds of remarks about his baldness in the earliest CBGB days, before Quine had the kind of reputation that would have made them more respectful.) When he showed up at the bookstore he'd already seen me in Television. He admired Television, and seeing us renewed his hope that there might actually be a place for him in modern music. He lived for raw, savvy rock and roll, but he hadn't been in a band since he was in law school in St. Louis in the late sixties.

We became good friends and I'd go over to his dark little studio apartment on St. Mark's Place and we'd listen to records and he'd shake us icy martinis.

His huge record collection contained mostly fifties rock and roll, as well as blues and R & B from their classic eras. There was also plenty of jazz, the most well represented being Miles Davis and Charlie Parker, along with all of Albert Ayler's recordings, and multiple disks by many other favorites, such as Bill Evans, Charlie Christian, Lee Konitz, Lester Young, and Lenny Tristano. He had multiple bootleg records of unreleased material by each of his favorite musicians too. He was much less interested in later, post-Beatles rock and roll, except for a few important exceptions like the Velvet Underground and the Stooges, along with some pet favorites like the Byrds (Roger McGuinn), and Jeff Beck and some Hendrix, and other guitar soloists, like Roy Buchanan and J. J. Cale and Harvey Mandel. And then he had countless albums that were not classifiable except that they were appreciated by Bob. The main thing though was that he didn't like nearly as much rock and roll or R & B that was made after the fifties as he liked the original gutbucket and heartfelt stuff. He loved Jimmy Reed and Link Wray, Ike Turner, Fats Domino, the Everly Brothers, Bo Diddley, Ritchie Valens and Buddy Holly and Little Richard.

Our tastes matched almost perfectly, except that he was so much more knowledgeable than me and he had practically no interest in Bob Dylan, or reggae, or much in country music except for Hank Williams (though he adored roots rockabilly), or, later, any modern "punk" bands at all (he did get off on some original sixties garage/punk, like, say, the Chocolate Watch Band, which he'd seen live, and the 13th Floor Elevators' first album). I myself didn't actually listen to punk music, like the Ramones and the Sex Pistols, for pleasure, but I liked and respected their albums, while he didn't. The aversion to reggae was especially mysterious, since that music is so wacky and homemade, the way Bob liked recordings, and Bob liked a lot of New Orleans rock and roll, and reggae comes out of a New Orleans beat. I think maybe these gaps of his came from his being guitar or solo oriented, which reggae and Dylan and country music and punk aren't. When I pressed him about it, he'd just be a wiseass. He was a fanatic for what grabbed him though. He had many many albums that he kept because of a single track, often a single twenty-five-second solo, or for only a single musician, like James Burton on Ricky Nelson tunes, John McVie's bass playing on Fleetwood Mac records, Joe Osborne's bass on even the worst cornball pop, or Grant Green's guitar on a lot of pretty trashy material.

By early 1976, when I was getting fed up with the Heartbreakers, I was feeling Bob out about my situation, and he was becoming fumblingly, modestly thrilled that he might conceivably get invited to join an interesting band. Eventually he played me a few tapes of his college groups doing covers of Chuck Berry and the Byrds and the Rolling Stones and the Velvet Underground, and that's what decided it. It was obvious he could do anything on guitar I'd dream of asking him to. As it turned out, he'd do a lot I didn't have the wherewithal to dream of yet.

Quine was an angry guy and the anger came from his being maltreated and dismissed by morons and thugs and tight-assed social conservatives, including his parents, for his whole life. His family was well-off and educated but straight. He never had anything nice to say about them. He'd been traumatized by the way he'd been a favorite object of maliciousness at boarding school, according to him. Doubtless that helped develop his cynical, taunting sense of humor. He grumbled about how his aged mother wasn't dying fast enough, or he'd sucker you into saying something out of politeness that he'd then mock you for, laughingly. At the same time he was humble. It was a point of honor with him not to claim more achievement than he'd attained and to always acknowledge the talents of others.

Quine was an angry guy

While he had a lot of interests outside of music, too, music came first by a huge margin. (Though he had no interest in classical music. When I discovered Beethoven's late piano sonatas, which sounded as wild and inspired as great jazz improvisations to me, I made a tape of them for him, and it left him cold.) He liked good writing. His favorite writers were Nabokov and Burroughs. He had Olympia Press first editions of both *Lolita* and *Naked Lunch*. He liked movies, especially dark and crude ones. He was both a big Sam Fuller fan and a Three Stooges fan. We bonded over Hugo Haas, a pet favorite film director of mine. Quine was the only guy I'd ever met who was into Haas, or even aware of him. And when Bob was interested in material, he not only learned everything about it but collected every example he could. He always collected—books, videotapes and then DVDs, albums and

CDs of course, and guitars. He bought guitars every year of his life starting as a teenager and he kept them immaculate. When he died he had upward of a hundred, almost all Fenders.

Quine was a misanthrope. He thought people were shits and cretins. His favorite words were probably "moron," "cretin," and "horrible." He couldn't suffer fools. (Unless they knew something about music and they kissed his ass. He was that needy. And unfortunately he more and more needed and found suppliers of that ass-kissing the older and more dissipated he got, and it got more and more harmful to his health.) But he did worship the musicians he admired, and he was a generous friend, though he had periods of rejecting nearly every friend he ever had, and he didn't have a high opinion of himself either. He was tense. He always had to resort to some chemical relief for that tension, whether booze or Valium or, finally, relatively late, heroin. He went to a shrink for most of his adulthood. (It always surprised me when he mentioned he was doing that. I would have thought he was too private and too proud to go to a shrink. He was too private and too proud to go to AA or NA when he was desperate to give up heroin.)

He walked like an R. Crumb character, with his shoulders slumped, looking oppressed, though also cold and fierce, if half-spooked. He almost always wore dark glasses (prescription), along with his rumpled cheap button-down shirt, innocuous sports coat, jeans, and generic Oxford shoes. He had a plain, anonymous, small-featured face that aged well. He didn't want to be noticed. I confronted him about that once. I asked him if he'd ever had a car, and when he said yes, I said I bet that it was either brown or gray. "It was brown!"

Despite all Bob's pride and bitterness, he was, in relation to me, primarily grateful and admiring, and he aimed to please. Initially, he was practically a dog. Getting plunged into the CBGB band scene must have been hard for him, if gratifying. It was the heart of rock and roll in the world at the moment, while also filthy dirty and sick, the way he liked it, while, on the other hand, he had no reputation and there were plenty of people at CBGB happy to insult or snub him. He also had to try to satisfy me when I had a hard time expressing what I wanted from him as a guitar player. I would insist on messing with his appearance as well. I made him grow stubble on his face and wear torn-up clothes.

I think Quine was the best rock and roll guitar soloist ever. He found a way to mix art with emotion that put him ahead of everyone. It's sad that he made so few recordings. His best playing was with me, and we made fewer than three albums' worth of material. There haven't really been many interesting guitar soloists in rock and roll. Mickey Baker, James Burton, Grady Martin, Link Wray, Jeff Beck, Jimi Hendrix, Lou Reed, maybe Jimmy Page, maybe Chuck Berry (he and Keith Richards and Pete Townshend are really rhythm players), maybe Tom Verlaine and Richard Thompson, and Quine. I don't know. (I'm leaving out blues musicians too.) No one has had the combination of creativity and feeling that Quine did. Most of the great rock and roll guitarists stand out for their wildness and momentum and humor, and that's plenty. It's suitable for the material. Quine brought feeling to the mix.

I've played with a lot of exceptional guitarists, but the thing I've noticed about nearly all of them compared to Quine is the gap between skillful creative brilliance and genius. Quine was a genius guitar player. He assumed as fundamental the qualities that were the highest aspirations of most soloists, and he would then depart from that platform into previously unknown areas of emotion and musical inspiration. He was a complicated, volatile, sensitive, very smart person who humbly channeled everything he was and knew into his guitar playing. It was axiomatic with him that emotion was the content created by the language of the musical instrument and the genre of the composition. Yes, he liked noise too, and subverting convention. That was the reveling, defiant, purely sound-oriented, unsentimental artist in him. And the antisocial one. But ultimately it was the depth of feeling, not any pioneering explorations or any technical facility or any kind of academic sophistication, that set him apart, just as was true of Miles Davis and Charlie Parker.

I've seen over the years how a person sometimes absorbs bits of behavior from friends—speech mannerisms or gestures. It can be eerie to recognize it in yourself after the friend has died. There was a thing Bob would do. Instead of smiling, he would just stretch his lips across his teeth in a cursory sign for "smile." His eyes wouldn't change at all, just his mouth for a moment. It was actually friendly—a signal that he was not unwilling to expend the energy to give a little reassurance. I catch myself doing that now and feel switched with Quine for a second.

Just when I'd left the Heartbreakers, before I'd formed a new band, I was approached about a management production deal by Marty Thau. Marty's main claim to fame was that he'd discovered, in his terms, and comanaged the Dolls prior to Malcolm's brief last-ditch attempt to save the band. Thau thought of himself as a hipster, though he looked like a thug and didn't mind exploiting that resemblance in order to intimidate when he could. He'd entered a partnership with Richard Gottehrer in a production company called Instant Records, to sign a young band or two. A production company functions to present a record label with a package that includes a record producer and often a band/artist's management as well as the musician(s). Gottehrer was a producer, former member of the sixties punk/garage band the Strangeloves ("Night Time" and "I Want Candy" —undeniably great cuts of their type), and original cofounder of Sire Records with Seymour Stein. He'd recently departed Sire. Marty was Instant's talent scout, and Gottehrer its businessman and record producer. Gottehrer was a tall, skinny, bulb-nosed, frizzy-haired guy who seemed good-natured, though aloof. He was all business. It was Marty who represented Instant to me at the beginning, though by the time I accepted Instant's proposal that we sign with Sire Records, he was out of the picture. Instant became solely Gottehrer. But originally Thau did the talking, as if he were the A & R guy. He wanted to hang out with me and smoke weed or snort cocaine.

Like most unsigned young musicians, I knew nothing about the record business. I was not only naïve but deluded. My idea of the recording artist's life came from *A Hard Day's Night* and *Don't Look Back*. I expected to travel in limousines for protection from screaming girls. It's not that I felt entitled or power-hungry (though, as much as I was affronted by rock royalty, I definitely wanted both lustful fans and people committed to carrying out my ideas otherwise), but that I assumed that the girls and cars just automatically accompanied record contracts. I didn't think about it. I was already making more money than I ever had before and also had more girls. And many people wanted to interview me. And I was full of ideas. It seemed like there was no limit to where it could all lead.

I was twenty-six by this time but it had been only three years since I'd first tried to play a bass and write a song, and I had first played in public less than a year after starting to learn. I was a high school dropout and relatively unworldly. Gottehrer and Thau were each about ten years older than me, and they were businessmen with long histories of scuffling (Thau) and hustling (Gottehrer) to profit from securing percentages of bands' earnings. Even Gottehrer's Strangeloves were nothing but a business project. The band hadn't actually existed, but was just whipped up as press releases to cash in on teen trends (kind of like Theresa Stern!). Strangeloves records were written and produced by a three-man production team that included Gottehrer but were played by hired studio musicians. The Strangeloves' public bio was a pure fabrication that presented them as brothers from Australian sheep-farm country. "I Want Candy" was a Bo Diddley riff with new bubble-gum-punk words and a dumbed-down production (like "Blank Generation" in relation to the "Beat Generation" novelty number, but kind of reversed in quality-switch!).

Thau similarly hacked bubble-gum music, but more as a salesman, for the teen-trash label Buddah (*sic*), before he started focusing on trying to profit from the New York underground scene, beginning with the Dolls. Both these biz scramblers came out of the tradition of Brill Building teen-music manufacture and the independent-label exploitation of starry-eyed young musicians.

I don't remember Gottehrer ever mentioning to me his former partnership with Seymour Stein of Sire. I found out about that later. In early 1976, just as I was forming the Voidoids but before we'd begun rehearsing, Instant offered me a deal in which they'd finance my band's demo tape and pay me $100 a week and a lesser amount to each of the other band members. Once the tape was complete, they'd have four months to get me a contract for an LP. In return for these services and investments, Instant would get approximately 50 percent of all record royalties paid the band by our future label. (My contract with Instant would pay me 7 percent of our first album's cover price as artist's royalties because we expected the record company deal would pay 14 percent of the cover price, meaning a fifty-fifty split between Gottehrer and me. As it worked out the Sire deal paid 12 percent, so Gottehrer got 5/12ths, which is 42 percent. This is still more than I was paid, since half my 7 percent went to my band. In other words, I earned 3.5 percent artist's royalties for the album, while Gotteherer earned 5 percent.) Instant would recoup all their investment (our salaries and the cost of the demo production) from off the top—the advance—of whatever record deal they could get us. I would have approval of any such prospective deal.

I didn't have any management or legal advice when considering this offer. It sounded OK to me. I figured how could I lose, given that Instant only had a few months to find me a deal or our agreement would expire, and I had approval of the terms of any proposed deal? On the other hand, Gottehrer got nearly half of the band's record royalties and I think the chances are pretty good that he knew all along that Sire, the label he'd cofounded with his friend Seymour, was pretty much a sure thing for us (in the previous months Sire had signed the Ramones and the Talking Heads, and would soon sign the Dead Boys). He even ended up sharing with Seymour Stein half the publishing royalties he was due, by my contract with Instant, from all the songs I wrote that are on my Sire album, *Blank Generation*. Since song-composition (as opposed to performance/recording artist's) royalties are divided equally between the writers and the publishers, that means that the pair of them were and are paid a combined total of 25 percent of the songs' royalties, for the entire life of the songs' copyrights.

Granted, all this is pretty typical, if unfair. I was innocent and ignorant, but at the same time, it's true that the most important thing to me was to make the record. The record business gangsters know this about young groups. I felt that as long as my basic needs were provided for, I was OK, knowing that all of these papers I was signing were limited in their duration anyway. They covered only the first few records and I figured I'd bring out a new record every year indefinitely.

The important thing was to get started. I didn't fully grasp that practically every cent invested in me by Gottehrer or the record company was an advance to me against future record royalties. None of the studio expenses or our salaries, etc., were finally paid by the record company; instead they were all recouped by the company from *my* share (as opposed to their share) of record royalties before I was paid any money in royalties. (It took something like seventeen years for me to get an artist's royalty check, apart from my original advance, from Sire.) This got pretty ironic. Sire switched distributors while I was recording my album, so they had to postpone its release for a few months. I was indignant and insisted that they compensate me for the delay by allowing me back in the studio to see if I could improve the performances of a few songs. I felt like a pretty important person when they agreed. But in fact *I* was the one paying for it anyway! (And God knows where the charges for studio time actually went.)

It's all normal capitalism. From Instant/Sire's point of view, they were gambling in the area of $50,000 on an album. If the album didn't earn anything, they were out that investment. They were going to do everything they could to be sure that the albums that did make money paid them big. But Thau (with whom I'd have further business dealings on my second album) and Gottehrer weren't really straight with me, by my lights. Eventually, twenty or thirty years later, I pursued them both with lawyers, going so far as to appear before a judge against Gottehrer, and was able to even the score fairly well, get some of my fair portion back. I don't respect or like either of them. They are typical of the record business—and the record business, notoriously, is one of the sleaziest there is. (Fredric Dannen, acclaimed investigative journalist of the business world, who'd also written about the mobster-dominated Teamsters Union, described the music business, in his book *Hit Men,* as the least ethical he'd ever seen.)

The ultimate advantage the music-racket honchos have over a guy like me is that they can afford to stall while my legal fees mount. Gottehrer, for instance, lives in a gigantic luxury apartment by the Natural History Museum, some of the toniest real estate in Manhattan, half a block from Central Park. The amounts of money I would be seeking to legally claim, from any given biz operator, rarely added up to more than an average of say $3,000–$5,000 a year, but could cost five or ten times that amount in lawyers' fees for me to recover. I am very lucky to have attorneys, Richard Golub and Nehemiah Glanc, who are not only fearsomely able, but who have often donated their services to me over the years out of friendship, and a sense of justice, and the goodness of their hearts.

As these business talks were beginning, there in the spring of 1976, the band was only Quine and me. I'd had my eye on drummer Marc Bell. He immediately agreed to quit Wayne County's sideshow group and join us. We rented a rehearsal studio to hold auditions for a second guitar player. I pretty much left it to Bob to assess the candidates for his guitar partner. We settled on Ivan Julian (original name: Ivan Parker) pretty quickly. Ivan was only twenty years old but had already been a professional guitar player for a while. He'd just returned from a tour of Europe playing with a journeyman late lineup of the Foundations ("Build Me Up Buttercup"). Ivan was a pro, was young and sharp, and he liked the same kind of slashing, swinging rhythm guitar that we did. He ended up playing some of the most popular and frenzied solos on our records as well.

So we started rehearsing, especially on the three songs we'd be recording as a demo for use in seeking an LP deal, which tracks were also going to be released as a limited-edition EP on Ork. The three songs were "Blank Generation," "You Gotta Lose," and a new one called "Another World." Ork Records was the independent outlet for 45s that Terry had started in order to get more circulation for the bands he cared about. The first release had been Television's "Little Johnny Jewel" in late 1975. My EP would be the second Ork record.

Richard Hell and the Voidoids, 1976.

visited Chris Stein and Debbie Harry one day up at Plaza Sound in Rockefeller Center, where they were recording the earliest Blondie tunes with Gottehrer. It was the summer of 1976. Chris was looking at a current European rock magazine, German or French. "Hey, Richard, you've got to see this. There are four guys who look exactly like you!" He showed me a color picture of a new band. I saw the band's name was the Sex Pistols. Good name too. I looked closer at the text and saw the words "Malcolm McLaren." His London clothing boutique was called Sex; hence Sex Pistols. I thought, "Malcolm really *did* like me." I had to laugh. Everybody in the band had short, hacked-up hair and torn clothes and there were safety pins and shredded suit jackets and wacked-out T-shirts and contorted defiant facial expressions. The lead singer had changed his name to something ugly. It gave me kind of a giddy feeling. It was flattering. It was funny. They looked great. I thought, "This thing is really breaking out."

Patti Smith's first LP, *Horses,* had been released at the end of 1975, just when I was about to leave the Heartbreakers, and her second album would come out a year later, in fall '76, when the Instant-backed Voidoids were debuting. The Ramones' first album had come out in the spring of '76. Neither their record nor Patti's was selling a lot but Patti was getting a good amount of publicity. Television and the

Talking Heads and Blondie would all be making label deals towards the end of 1976 and so would my new band. It was a high time, but the advent of the Sex Pistols upped the ante and made people reassess. News started coming through heavily in the second half of the year.

Since the sixties, rock and roll bands had been all that England had to be proud of (even though those sixties bands had started as imitations of American rock and roll too), so music was a major focus there. The country had three popular national weekly music papers—*Melody Maker*, *New Musical Express*, and *Sounds*. Though the U.S. had well over three times the population of the UK, and American bands were just as successful worldwide and just as interesting, we had only *Rolling Stone* for broad national rock and roll news coverage, and it came out half as often as those English papers and was comparatively conservative. It did not routinely cover what was going on in clubs in New York or L.A., while the British papers always wrote about new unsigned UK bands. Furthermore, because England was small, whatever happened in London was instantly national news, while, though the CBGB bands had become the talk of haute New York, that didn't make them newsworthy in Kansas.

As things picked up speed, it was hard to accept that the groundwork we'd laid was paying off big for complete strangers, and strangers who seemed hostile to us. But the most frustrating thing was that they were so good. Rotten's interviews were breathtaking. He mocked and hated everything. He was the opposite of the usual eager-to-impress, humble aspiring celebrity. Rock and roll is about subverting respectability, but there'd never been a musician who so blatantly and fully didn't give a shit, who just wanted to mix things up and undermine expectations. He actually said his band's mission was to destroy rock and roll. That was fucking incomparable.

I'd written and performed a song in Television in 1974 called "Fuck Rock and Roll" but the song wasn't rock and roll, it was distorted, defaced rock and roll, and free jazz—a challenge. The Sex Pistols said "fuck rock and roll" but in the most blistering, rampaging rock and roll songs. I'd written and sung blistering rock and roll too, though another one of my songs, "Blank Generation," one that would inspire the Sex Pistols to write their song "Pretty Vacant," was performed in a more laid-back and dreamy, if sarcastic and sneering, style, until the Pistols upped the ante in undiluted rock and roll the way they did, and I started playing "Blank Generation" in a more aggressive style too.

I'd also given deeply nihilistic interviews before the Sex Pistols had been heard of, but mine was a lot more self-conscious than Rotten's negativity. My very first individual interview was with Legs McNeil for *Punk* magazine, and was conducted when I was in the Heartbreakers, in late 1975, before the Sex Pistols had appeared. I'd said, in a booth with Legs at Max's Kansas City:

> "Basically I have one feeling, and that's this little voice in my head. Well I mean the one main feeling I have is the desire to get out of here. And any other feelings I have come from trying to analyse why I want to go away. . . . It's not going to any other place or any other sensation or anything like that. It's just to get out of 'here.'"
>
> "Where do you feel comfortable?"
>
> "When I'm asleep."
>
> "How many pairs of underwear do you have?"
>
> "One."

"One? How long have you had them?"

"I bought a pair of underwear because I had so many holes in my pants it became necessary. But now I have so much holes in my underwear it hardly makes any difference."

"Why do you wear ripped up clothes? Did you rip them up?"

"I did rip one shirt once but I sewed it back together because I felt guilty . . . I knew a guy like you once. He tried to fuck a transvestite and almost got his balls cut off and ended up in an insane asylum."

"Have you ever fallen in love?"

"I think love is sort of a con you play on yourself. I think the whole conception of love is something the previous generation invents to justify having created you. You know I think the real reason children are born is because parents are so bored they have children to amuse themselves. They're so bored they don't have anything else to do so they have a child because that will keep them busy for a while. Then to justify to the kid the reason he exists they tell him there's such a thing as love and that's where you come from because me and your daddy or me and your mommy were in love and that's why you exist. When actually it was because they were bored out of their minds."

"Are you glad you were born?"

"I have my doubts."

"Were you a gigolo?"

"I think that rock and roll is being a gigolo. It's trying to convince girls to pay money to be near you."

There's not too much precedent, in its antisociability and funny negativity and twisted honesty, for an interview like that with a rock and roll musician, but Rotten was more compelling. I was an off-putting navel-gazer by comparison. Rotten was all energy and extroversion. He galvanized the kids. I was the opposite, a sullen forlorn junkie outcast who just wanted to be left alone, except by admiring girls. He was about the whole world; I was about myself. I did imagine myself as a visionary whose sensibility and ideas would change everything, or at least represent this new generation, but I also knew that this was implausible. How many kids were going to get excited about calling themselves "blank"? The concept of "anarchy" was just as disgusted and contrary but a lot more fun.

Furthermore I hadn't really figured out how to make the music sound the way I wanted it to. My music could be halting and intellectual and difficult, and sometimes half-baked. The style and sound I eventually arrived at for my first album was rich but idiosyncratic. Furthermore, I didn't want a signature sound; I wanted every song to be different from every other song. In a sense I'd passed through my punk period with the Neon Boys and early Television, with relentless driving expressions of attitude like "That's All I Know (Right Now)," "I'm Nice," "Change Your Channel," the original version of "Love Comes in Spurts," and the twisted seminovelty of "Fuck Rock and Roll" and "Blank Generation." Then there was the more power-punk New Yorkabilly hardass sneering of the Heartbreakers. Now, with the new band, the music had become more eccentric and complex, often misshapen.

When the Voidoids first started rehearsing, my top priorities were to whip the band into a team by talking about what set us apart and thinking about how we'd present ourselves physically. I wasn't sure of what to call the band yet. A list of possible names I made then:

The Scream
The Statues
The Savage Statues
The Sleep
The Junkyard
The Drool
The Droolers
The Morons
The Homicides
The Hyenas
The Haloes
The Hinges
The Hazard
The Dogbites
The Facial Expressions
The Ineffables
The Beauticians
The Teeth

I like those, especially "The Beauticians." Typically, I ended up choosing the most difficult name I thought of.

From the beginning the Voidoids were a locus, a center and source of New York music. It was what I'd been waiting for, what I'd been working towards since I'd first picked up a bass and started writing and singing songs.

At CBGB my accomplishments were known and I was a leader of the new sensibility. Patti was the only other writer/performer/conceptualist/bandleader who rivaled me in that way. She was more charismatic than me and a better performer and drew bigger crowds, but she was also full of shit in many ways, and a hypocritical, pandering diva, and her band was generic and mediocre.

I was full of shit in many ways too, and self-important, and uneven musically, but I had endless ideas and vision that had been central to shaping everything that went into making up the culture and style, musical and otherwise, of CBGB, and naturally that music and culture and style excited me, since I had been responsible for originally expressing a lot of it, and just as naturally that culture liked me back. I sometimes felt like the king of the Lower East Side, and I was, in meaningful respects, though I was also aware that the crown was mine largely by virtue of my appreciation of the realm and because I hated royalty.

CHAPTER TWENTY-THREE

W e all read Lester Bangs when he wrote for *Creem* in the early seventies. You had to love him even though, in person, his musical fanaticism was a little embarrassing. He was not cool; he babbled and raved, and treated music as if it were the center of the universe. On the other hand, he was the definition of cool in that his taste and judgment were so advanced as to practically qualify him as a great musician himself, especially in view of how his writing was so searching and honest and full of imagination. He was the rare music writer who actually seemed more interested in the music than in himself. That moment, when Lester came to New York from Detroit in 1976, was the last time that rock criticism really came from the heart (I guess that makes the heart Detroit). Lester was the last critic to stake his life on music. (Though Robert Palmer is up there too . . .)

I didn't have much patience for him at the time, though. He was a shameless drunk and pill head. He always wanted to talk and ask me questions. He wanted to leap right into metaphysics and sociology. That's the difference between a musician and a critic—the musician makes semiabstract little material expressions and resolutions of the noise in his brain and body, while the critic wants to theorize and argue about those results. Furthermore, though I was a guy who liked to think and analyze to a certain extent, I didn't want to do it with a journalist, who was in the position of taking what I said and framing it in his own terms, distorting it, and making that public. Which is what happened when I agreed to talk to Lester.

Lester was fascinated by, and devoted to, the Voidoids for two main reasons. One was Quine's talent and taste—Quine and Lester were a perfect match, though Bob would also lose patience with Lester's dipsomaniacal sincerity. But they loved each other, and Lester was one of the very few who fully appreciated what Quine could do on guitar. The other reason Bangs was impressed by us was because of my commitment to emotional and technically/aesthetically extreme music, but, even more, he was attracted by the meanings in songs that said things like "Love comes in spurts" and "Who says it's good to be alive?" and "I belong to the _____ generation."

It's ironic how Bangs's belief in us, and his compulsion to understand what was going on in the music that interested him, would contribute to the single most significant misbegotten interpretation of my intentions. It occurred when he provoked me to say something that has ever since been waved around by anybody who's referred to the song "Blank Generation" in print.

The problem stems from an interview piece Lester published in late 1977 called "Richard Hell: Death Means Never Having to Say You're Incomplete." It flatters me as a prophet ("Richard Hell is one of the poets. . . . And because he's one of the few thinkers I respect . . ."), and praises me as a musician too ("one of the greatest rock 'n' rollers I have ever heard"), but Lester had come into the meeting arguing with himself and he ended up projecting one side of that argument on me.

He asked me, "Isn't so much of the punk movement involved with self-hatred?" and I went, "There's a lot of basis for self-hatred. To transcend something you've got to fully accept the fact that it exists. I would much rather listen to the music of somebody who hates himself and says it than listen to the music of Barry Manilow."

When he asked me whether the idea in "Love Comes in Spurts" that "love" is a lie leads to nasty narcissism, I told him, "One thing I wanted to bring back to rock and roll was the knowledge that you invent yourself. That's why I changed my name, why I did all the clothing style things, the haircut, everything. So naturally, if you invent yourself, you love yourself. The idea of inventing yourself is creating the most ideal image that you could imagine. So that's totally positive."

Despite those kinds of explanations, Lester ended up writing, "Look, I started out saying how much I *respected* this guy's mind and perceptions. I still do in a curious way—it's just that he paints half the picture of reality with consummate brilliance, and the other half is Crayola slashes across a field of Silly Putty and Green Slime. [. . .] His whole picture is a self-fulfilling prophecy—he has designed his world in such a way that things ought to work out every bit as miserably as he expects." Nearly everything I'd said specifically contradicts all that. (Another irony is that his line about brilliance with slashes of Crayola, Silly Putty, and Slime is maybe my favorite way I've ever seen my work described—it's my aesthetic ideal!)

The ultimate problem, though, came from how I saw from the beginning of the interview that he wanted to portray me as childishly negative, and so I told him, "People misread what I meant by [the song] 'Blank Generation.' To me, 'blank' is a line where you can fill in anything. It's positive. It's the idea that you have the option of making yourself anything you want, filling in the blank." That's legitimate, but I was playing it up to head off Lester's making me out as all anti-life. When people insist on narrowing down or overinterpreting what you're doing, the reflex is to point out other perspectives. Artists do that all the time. Dylan refers to himself as a song-and-dance man. Andy Warhol says there's nothing beneath his surface.

But the result has been that, ever since, no one has been able to write about "Blank Generation" without saying that I insist it's not about being numb or empty but about having infinite possibilities.

I was saying "Let me out of here" before I was
even born. It's such a gamble when you get a face.
It's fascinating to observe what the mirror does,
but when I dine it's for the wall that I set a place.

I belong to the blank generation
and I can take it or leave it each time.
I belong to the _____ generation
but I can take it or leave it each time.

Does that sound joyous with the opportunities for self-realization? The vocal is anguished and furious too. Would I really write "I belong to the blank generation" without knowing that it would be understood as describing us as being numb and apathetic? That would be like thinking I could say "I belong to the gay generation" when I meant that I felt happy a lot. The meaning of the song is its ambivalence and ambiguity. Another of its little mechanisms is the way that the first line of the refrain says, "I belong to the blank generation, and I can take it or leave it each time," while the repetition goes "*but* I can take it or leave it each time." So, in other words, the ambivalence is so profound that even the ambivalence itself can be taken or left.

Anya Phillips was at CBGB every spare minute she had. She was a stripper in a midtown club who performed as "Peking Doll," and she was devoted to me and our band. She founded a Voidoids fan club in 1976. She was Asian—Taiwanese American—and had grown up with her best friend, Sylvia Morales, out in the Asian Pacific, where their fathers were in the military. Sylvia ended up marrying Lou Reed and living with and managing him for a long time. Anya eventually managed and mentored James Chance, poster boy of the no wave.

Anya was known for being smart and tough. She was a professional dominatrix as well as the controller of the quiet, subdued James, who broke out of his shell onstage. But her relationship with me was the opposite of controlling. Like other young girls who hung out at CBGB in those early days, such as Nancy Spungen and Lydia Lunch, she loved the world of the club and entered it completely. And to Anya the club's primary identity was as my platform, and I represented what mattered about the world of the club. To me, she also was not exactly a person but the embodiment of a function. She was a girl who wanted to be

Anya with James Chance.

around me and who, by that equation, I was always some steps beyond. She put herself in this position. But she was not exactly a "groupie"; she was more like an apprentice. She would do as I pleased because she wanted to please me, but also in exchange for hearing what I might have to say about things and for seeing how I behaved. This is not to say that I abused her or disrespected her; the exchange between us was fair and was the only relationship possible, given her presentation of herself to me.

Her apartment was on the ground floor on East Tenth Street. It was a cool gray cell, lightless, bare, and remote. When I wanted I went over there and she gave me money. I would go acquire a few bags of heroin, bring them back, and we would experience sex. The heroin was a reward for our status as outsider artists. This was innocent and quiet. At that time it was innocent. She followed my instructions and she was always glad about where they led. I remember closing my eyes and gathering my mind as if it were an armful of wood and depositing it on the "stoned" pile. We were members of a particular race, a secret race, quiet and aware. Kind of beat up, but strong. Access to her body was just as complete and uncomplicated as well.

I haven't mentioned Peter Laughner yet either. Like Anya and Lester, he wasn't in a New York band but was connected to the scene—in Peter's case he actually was a musician, but he lived in Cleveland, Ohio, and that's where his bands played. He visited New York as often as he could from 1975 until his death in 1977, and he cultivated New York friends and contacts at CBGB. He'd already made friends with Lester, by writing to him at *Creem,* before Lester came to New York. Peter was one of the founders of the interesting cold-ass industrial band Pere Ubu, but he remained with them only long enough to play on their first single. He played in and was largely responsible for creating the earlier group Rocket from the Tombs, which was the basis for not only Pere Ubu but the Dead Boys.

Laughner was self-destructive, smart, a natural-born guitar player, and grew from the same roots—the Velvet Underground especially—as the CBGB bands. Lester and Anya and Peter exemplified something that was new about CBGB in rock and roll—and what set it apart from the British scene it sparked—in that they were intellectual. They were interested in ideas and liked to talk and think. (Malcolm did too—he was an exception in England.) Anya wasn't a philosopher, but she was observant and analytical and she respected thought and insight, even if she could be a sneering bitch (in the best sense of the words). Lester and his friend Peter were literate and interested in ideas, unlike, say, Sid Vicious, or the moronic, hypocritical British journalo-sheep, such as

With Peter Laughner.

Tony Parsons and Julie Burchill, who, like party functionaries in Mao's Cultural Revolution, mocked Americans for reading books. (Mocking books is OK. Books are a hobby, are a taste, like anything else. God knows we mocked the Brits. Their hobby seemed to be potatoes. They might not have liked books, but they loved a spud. Fried potato sandwiches. The countless English storefronts serving spuds and spuds only. Every vile dead block its potato shop.)

Peter was actually probably less fun and interesting to be with than Sid. Wait, that's not true . . . There's not much point in comparing the two. I guess the main difference in them as avatars of a kind of punkness, apart from what I've already mentioned, is that Sid stayed infantile and clownish in his fucked-upness, while Peter was more melodramatic and bitter about it. In that way Sid was a newer type and more purely "punk." Peter had ideas and musical talent but Sid didn't pretend to either of those things. Both of their stories are sad and demoralizing. And what one has to say about either one of them has to do with one's mood and whom one is talking to. Because it's about the sadness of life, about suffering, about hopelessness; sometimes one takes that seriously and sometimes one doesn't.

There was an inherent contradiction in rock and roll for me. On one hand I wanted to do it because it was physical and unhinged; on the other, I wanted to use my brain to make the songs say as much as possible and to exploit every other aspect of having a band to say as much as possible too, as interestingly as possible. I was not any kind of intellectual snob—I was a high school dropout for a reason—but at the same time I wasn't ashamed of my interest in books and in thinking, and even wanted to affirm that, just to make a point, America being so idiotically anti-intellectual. I felt secure enough in my credentials as the real thing in rock and roll to be able to refer to Gertrude Stein or Nietzsche or Nerval in interviews. I wanted to reconcile the physical and intellectual, and be seen doing it. But almost always people disregarded or misunderstood (or made fun of) one side or the other (or both!) of what I was doing along those lines.

Peter Laughner liked to think about things, and analyze them, too, but he was also a natural-born musician (unlike me) as well as being the most self-destructively drug-hungry drunk of all the many I've known. He just flatly yielded, no resistance, to his impulses to take drugs and drink, the way anyone else would scratch their nose when it itched. Methedrine seemed to be his preference, but alcohol was always present, and he took downs and codeine too. He wrote songs about Sylvia Plath and Baudelaire, as well as one called "Life Stinks," and, with the Dead Boys' Cheetah Chrome, the sarcastic "Ain't It Fun," which Guns N' Roses later performed on their album of punk covers.

He made a solo cassette tape in his room at his parents' house, accompanying himself on acoustic guitar and harmonica, on what turned out to be suddenly, unexpectedly, the night his years of chemical self-abuse caught up with him and he died there in his bed of acute pancreatitis. It was 1977 and he was twenty-four and still living at home. The tape, labeled by him "Nocturnal Digressions," is mostly others' material, and he doesn't sound well, but he plays and performs heart-rendingly. On the tape he calls "Blank Generation" his favorite recent lyric, and he plays it as well as Television's "See No Evil," and songs by Richard Thompson ("The Calvary Cross"), The Rolling Stones ("Wild Horses"), Robert Johnson ("Me and the Devil Blues"), the Velvets ("Pale Blue Eyes"), Eddie Cochran ("Summertime Blues"), and seven or eight more.

When I knew him in New York I didn't know about his talent but only his drunken fanaticism. In retrospect his story is familiar but still it moves me. In the mideighties, when I'd left music (and drugs) and was first attempting to figure out how to write for a living, I got *Spin* magazine to send me to Cleveland to investigate Laughner's life. A few things became clear: the quality of his taste and talent; the depth of his self-doubt and concomitant surrender to drugs and other means of self-escape (including sexual sadomasochism); and his generosity (he encouraged, and improved the lives of, many people in Cleveland). He was so pure and so tainted at once. He gave people joy and tore them up. His songs held nothing back, but that could make them silly too ("Sylvia Plath / was never too good at math / but they tell me that she finished at the head of her clath").

The week I spent in Cleveland interviewing those who'd known him, I thought about nothing but Laughner, and that was harrowing and complicated. On the last day I was there I went by myself to visit his grave. I knew that his parents, who'd doted on him—he was an only child who was born relatively late in their lives—had had his gravestone engraved "play on, beloved son." It took me a while to find the plot. The marker was a small panel laid flush to the earth. Snowflakes were falling sparsely. As I stood there, thoughts and feelings about Laughner rushed through my mind in a ghostly torrent, impossible to read, and I was too tired and fed up to try to sort it out anyway. Then, in my extreme mixed feelings, which were largely composed of exhaustion and impatience with all the emotional information, and without quite realizing what I'd done until I had, I spat on his grave.

CHAPTER TWENTY-FOUR

T he Voidoids debuted, at CBGB, in the fall of 1976. The year that followed was the peak of my career in music. I still remembered what I was there for and I had the means to express it. One could say I'd been good, as well as happy, for five minutes in the Neon Boys/Television and ten minutes in the Heartbreakers, and I would be happy and good for twenty minutes in the Voidoids.

I'd been approached by Instant in April 1976, just when I was deciding to leave the Heartbreakers. I'd signed with the production company and then spent May gathering, with Quine, the new band. The Voidoids started rehearsing in June, and at the end of that month we recorded the three-song demo that would be our first release. That raw, clunky Ork Records EP of "Blank Generation," "Another World," and "You Gotta Lose" was released in late November. We debuted live in November also, at CBGB. We got an offer from Sire Records two months later, in January 1977, and negotiated an agreement with them by mid-February. We started recording the album in March, and after a delay, caused by Sire's switching its distribution from ABC to Warner, the album came out in October 1977.

The band rehearsed steadily that first year, organizing arrangements and working up new songs. I'd only brought the group a few numbers, because I'd cowritten many of my songs with former bandmates and I didn't want to use those. I had "Blank Generation" and "Love Comes in Spurts," and a sketch of "New Pleasure," but most of the album was written in the nine months before recording it.

I had "You Gotta Lose," but it was too retro to keep high in the repertoire—too Chuck Berry and rockabilly. I always liked its lyrics though. I wrote them partly about Verlaine—the start of the second verse—right after I left Television, using my dissonant bass line from the Neon Boys' "High Heeled Wheels." Verlaine was someone who would never admit to a mistake, as if it was unacceptable to ever be wrong or to fail at anything. I hated that attitude. In fact I thought life was pretty much a losing proposition, and I didn't mind saying so.

I hope I don't seem immodest when I tell you that my my
mother was a pinhead and my father was a fly.
That's why I love you darling with a love that's so unique—
your glistenin wings they complement your head's exquisite

peak.

They all died by coin toss.
Love's a form of memory loss.
I can't forget that triple cross. . .

You gotta lose, you gotta lose. . .

Not too long ago I knew a guy who thought he can't be beat
but he got rabies on his rubies now he can't unlace his feet.
And I for twenty minutes yesterday felt great felt insensate
but when you're twenty minutes late your fate is patient and

will wait.

[Chorus]

I know it's hard for you to face the fact Max Factor failed your
                                                                    face
and that your social life's misshapen cuz you feel so out of place
and that the most magic man you'd meet and ask your soul to
                                                                    keep
still could only love you from a distance one man deep.

[Chorus]

By the time the Voidoids signed with Sire I was a drug addict,
though I didn't even fully realize it. I'd feel bad if I didn't have
heroin, but the bad feeling was not much worse than a touch of the
flu, and I could go without using and still be able to get around
for days before it became too maddening. What had begun as an
occasional vacation with Ork in the Television days had become a
regular routine in the Heartbreakers, and by 1977 I was using a bag
or two every day.

Then I discovered methadone. Methadone was the drug the fed-
eral government gave addicts who registered at clinics. It satisfied
heroin need, and if you had to hunker down and take care of business, controlled doses of methadone let you handle yourself as if you
were straight. That's all I knew, and I assumed that methadone was not
habit-forming. It didn't occur to me that the government would give
out a drug to cure heroin addiction that was itself addictive. I thought
I had beaten the game when I got my methadone connection. In fact
methadone lingers in the system longer and produces worse withdrawal
symptoms than heroin. The main difference is that it ostensibly lets the
government control how you go about getting a maintenance level of

narcotics, while it also blocks the effect of heroin without itself providing a heroin rush. It's supposed to civilize an addict.

I got my methadone from a guy named Fernando, who was the super in the building next door to mine. He and his wife scored a couple of bottles at a government clinic twice a week and they only needed half of their supply. You had to take it orally. It was a powder suspended in orange drink and came in fifty-to-one-hundred-or-so-milligram portions in squat translucent plastic bottles with Day-Glo orange labels.

Fernando was a second-generation Puerto Rican–American and lived with his Anglo common-law wife, Karen, on the fifth floor of the tenement next door. They really tried to be respectable. I guess the methadone program was effective in that regard in their case. Their linoleum-floored apartment was spick and span, though it reeked thickly of cleaning fluids and stale cooking.

Both our apartments were on the fifth floors of our buildings, and his windows looked right into mine across the air shaft. Once he asked me in a mature, neighborly way to please not do that again to my girlfriend up against the kitchen sink, because his wife shouldn't see it. But there were advantages to the proximity too. I realized we had a set of windows close enough that I could reach across the corner of the air shaft to his window with a mop handle. So, to save the energy of going downstairs, climbing up to his apartment, and then dragging myself back, I rigged a mop handle with a paper bag rubber-banded to its end so he could switch the $12 inside for a methadone bottle. That little bottle would last me a good four days. I would have needed $60 or $80 worth of dime-bag heroin to last that long.

The routine was like a number in a movie musical, like *An American in Paris* or *Funny Face*. I, the male lead, never miss a pretty slide-step as

I glide around the living room preparing the pole, slip currency into the crumpled bag rubber-banded to its tip, pirouette to the next room's window, swoop the mop stick up across the air-shaft pit, and then wait a moment, quizzically, like a baby bird, or Fred Astaire foot-tapping to a tuneless whistle with his arms crossed, while grumpy, smudged, brown-Afro-ed Fernando tightly smiles, removing the cash to pop in the odd little methadone container. I pull back the pole, retrieve my prize, imbibe a sip, and drop onto the couch to relish a cold can of Coke and the *New York Times*, in advance of the onset of cure-all internal glow. My future assured, all is serene, as the music fades, camera pulls back, and the shot dissolves . . .

I had two or three girlfriends at this time. There were Lizzy and Sabel, and then later in the year Kate Simon for a while. Kate was unusual among my friends for being professional and mature. She was a rock photographer who'd lived in London and did a lot of work for *Sounds*. She had slanted Modigliani eyes, high cheekbones—concave cheeks like a model—a padded lower lip, thick stiff shoulder-length dark hair, a slim body with wide hips, and she walked splay-footed. She was pale and she didn't wear much makeup except lines of dark pencil around her eyes. I could make her laugh. People knew I did heroin, but doing heroin at that point was still kind of mysterious. It didn't signify crime and deceit and betrayal. When you're young enough you can get away with anything. Kate was smart and was in on the secret that some animalistic aggressive rock and roll musicians weren't morons either. We also worked well together in photo sessions.

I remember lying next to her on a mattress on the floor in the back bedroom in her bright, high-ceilinged, uptown photo-studio apartment and feeling guilty, knowing that, as knowledgeable and worldly and self-possessed as she was, she didn't understand that I wasn't good for her, that I had other allegiances. When I left her it hurt her and made her angry and she didn't really forgive me. I didn't treat her right. She wound up marrying David Johansen of the Dolls a few years later and they were together for decades.

The Voidoids spent three weeks making the record at Electric Lady, the subterranean flying saucer of a recording studio that Jimi Hendrix had built for himself on Eighth Street, a fifteen-minute walk from my apartment.*

As I said, the songs were in progress. There were missing lyrics and half-baked arrangements. I was writing lyrics in the studio and we experimented with tempos and backup vocals and solos.

I knew nothing about singing except that it was about emotion, and I had some instincts about the way to convey emotion rhythmically and in tones. For me, singing was like throwing something as hard as I could to stop a threat in its tracks, or stating something beyond a doubt to reassure someone whose confidence I needed, as if everything depended on it. I was aware that position and timing mattered, but I relied on instinct and subconsciously absorbed experience

---

* Twenty or so years later, I was given an LP by a friendly local used-record dealer who said that he'd had it since he was a teenager and that it led to his devotion to New York punk. It was a copy of Hendrix's double *Electric Ladyland* album, except side two of it was actually side two of the *Blank Generation* album. You could see how there could have been a mix-up at the factory—"Hendrix" and "Hell" are close alphabetically, but probably more importantly the Hendrix album's catalog number was 6307 while *Blank*'s was 6037. My friend insisted that he played the record for months thinking it was all Hendrix and that the Voidoids' side was his favorite of the four. Eventually I gave the double album to Ivan Julian. I've never heard of the existence of another copy.

to achieve them. And the power came not from volume, in decibels, but from emotion, in revelation. I had to be accurate not in pitch, but in emotional import, of which pitch was a subcategory. There was something mystical or at least irrational about the process. I had to trust that I could do it even though it required so much release. It was like being in an extended firefight, a fierce exchange in which life was threatened but that slowed time so it was still possible to take care. I depended on the band both to keep me on my feet and to compensate for my weaknesses.

My other major project was Quine. At this time he was pretty insecure, while remaining angry, as ever, under the surface. He tended to play more safely than I wanted. My songs were unusual and it wasn't clear what I expected from him exactly, so he tended to stay inside the bounds he could see in the patterns of the songs. Quine is now so highly respected a musician that it's probably hard to imagine how we worked together, considering how much less musically educated I was. Bob had even gone to Berklee for a while, but in our band he was subordinate to me, and that was natural, and accepted by him without resentment or reservation. As musically sophisticated as he was, he knew that rock and roll was not about sophistication, but about instincts and attitude and style. He knew that I was the leader of the band not just because I had built a local reputation, but because I was the engine and identity of the group, and had to be.

Having said that, he also knew how much I appreciated him. When I hear some of those recordings, they come to life during his solos and subside a bit afterwards.

Often, he didn't want to risk interfering with any possibility of a song. Also, as extreme as his tastes could be, he was a restrained person, and playing really well requires a level of abandon. I would push him and push him, basically infuriate him, and he sometimes hated me for it, but eventually he was glad. He told me so many times in later years. It also helped that he was not well respected by all the authorities—by the record company and by Gottehrer. It wasn't that they insulted him, they just didn't treat him with any specific respect. Because of that, he secreted venom that pooled inside and fueled his playing.

People still always ask me what the song "Blank Generation" means. If I trust them, I might tell them it was partly a joke, a joke that was meant to be understood by people compatible enough with me to get the joke, being that it was also a personal ad addressed to those "people compatible enough." But it was also a description of a state of consciousness that came from having lived through what people my age had lived through: the Vietnam War, the inevitable failure of the flower children, the exposed corruption and venality of the politicians, the sleaziness of patriotism, the flood of drugs, and the overwhelming media data flow of the late sixties and early seventies. That had been numbing and alienating, but, yes, in wearing away all your illusions, it did leave you in a place where the option of remaking yourself from scratch did come to mind. But really the song was an evasion of explanation, as most all attempts to write something decent are. Inevitably it was a self-portrait, still. "I was saying let me out of here before I was even born," it began.

The cover of the album showed another use of the "blank" concept. I'd arranged for a photo session with Roberta to get a shot for it. (Kate did some with the full band, but we ended up using that version on the back.) We took the pictures at Chris and Debbie's loft on the Bowery where there was some space. As usual at photo sessions, I tried to mul-

222

Blank Generation album original cover shot.

tiply the possibilities by shifting my clothing and props from shot to shot—with and without shirt or jacket, with and without sunglasses, etc. I also had the idea of writing something across my naked chest in black marker. I had to have Roberta print the words—"YOU MAKE ME _____"—across my chest, which I showed by holding open my raggedy suit coat. That's what I used on the cover. I liked the way the message of the sentence was underscored by the blank. And the way the statement both blamed the world ("you") for making "me" "blank" (or simply making me) and simultaneously offered "you" (the person looking at the album) the chance to turn that person on the cover from _____ into whatever else you might be inclined to make him by filling in the blank. Plus there's the challenge, like drawing a line in the sand ("Oh yeah? You make me").

Though they slipped a few things past me, the word at Sire was that I was to be accommodated. I made the final decisions about the playing and recording in the studio, and the record company also deferred to me regarding press releases and album art and, to a certain degree, advertising. They figured I was best positioned to know what might be consistent with the weirdness of the "new wave" we represented.

When I decided on the "YOU MAKE ME _____" photo for the album cover, I asked the Sire art department to transform the brick wall in the background of the shot into a flat blank flesh color, and I scrawled and scratched the album title and band name, RICHARD HELL & THE VOIDOIDS BLANK GENERATION, to stretch across the upper inch of the cover.

Lester Bangs later contributed an entry to *The Rolling Stone Book of Rock Lists* that named the top ten worst album covers in history "by major bands." Mine was number one. Lester always tried to give me my due.

Things were becoming strange. I'd arrived as a rock and roll singer, songwriter, and front man by desire and taste and analysis. I had evolved a conception of what the underlying reality of my time and location was and I was excited to transmit it in rock and roll. On the other hand I didn't really care; in fact that feeling was part of the foundation of my point of view and my message. ("I Don't Care" was actually one of the first songs I conceived for Television. Tom and Lloyd and I would each sing one verse. Tom dropped it from the repertoire pretty quickly. Later the Ramones did a different song with that title.) I'd just as soon have been alone. This created a kind of paradox. If your message is that you don't care about things, how can it be delivered? Where's the initiative? Even though I didn't fully understand this contradiction consciously, I intuited it. And its ruinous consequences were becoming more and more obvious.

When I look back at my behavior, my self-regard and self-centeredness, at that time, as evidenced in interviews, I'm embarrassed. I took myself pretty seriously. I thought I was smart. In my defense, I did try to be honest, and I questioned everything. But I was full of myself.

The problem with 1977 was that things stopped being about anticipation and potential and started becoming fixed reality, becoming history. I had to try to make my album equal the range of my phantom perceptions and projections. I felt lonely or at least solitary and I was impatient.

For nearly the entire time I was a professional musician, I chose ignorance. I depended on instinct and attitude rather than technical knowledge. I regarded myself as a force of nature and an entity worthy of sustained attention. I wrote and sang the songs and projected them via my physical self, and played bass, and it was the band's purpose to follow my lead in providing an appropriate setting and accompaniment. They were there to help construct the space consistent with me, a musical atmosphere I could breathe, in which I could act and carry out my intentions. That action took place in the medium of music but it was actually something else, a kind of aliveness. I could hear its incarnation in music, but it was the aliveness that was the purpose of the rock and roll. I know more than this now and I know how the record suffered for that approach of mine, but at the same time, it couldn't have been otherwise, so fuck it. It made for some great moments.

CHAPTER TWENTY-FIVE

─────────────────────────────────────

Sire's idea to promote the LP was to send us on a tour of England opening for the Clash. We would play twenty-one dates in twenty-three days in twenty cities. It was the first time I'd ever left the United States and the first time the band had ever played outside of New York.

England made a bad impression. It seemed defeated and ashamed. Its more privileged youth manifested this in continuous cynical, self-deprecating irony. Older people were still fixated, amazingly, on World War II, which was apparently the most recent moment in which they could take any pride. Everyone still seemed psychologically crushed by the collapse of the empire fifty years before.

Physically, it was more of the same. The streets of the East Village were burnt out and lawless, but they were Joyland compared to the death row oppressiveness of urban Britain. A lot of its streets were ugly for having been cheaply and tastelessly rebuilt after the World War II blitz bombings, but even the nineteenth-century blocks were endlessly monotonous, like misshapen penitentiaries.

For food there was fried potatoes, and potatoes and beans, and potatoes and eggs, and meat-potato pies and boiled potatoes.

The country was in even worse economic shape than New York City, without New York's cultural compensations. The lives of the working-class kids were especially miserable. There were no jobs for them and nothing to look forward to and nothing to do but beat each other up at soccer games.

This was the scene into which the Sex Pistols had exploded in the previous months. They'd overturned things not just with their maniacal rock and roll, but by the way their rage and sarcastic snottiness expressed British kids' frustration. There had never been rock and roll songs that literally advocated anarchy or screamed about how there was no future. Johnny Rotten said and did things the kids hadn't even known they'd felt, much less that it was possible to say, and they really loved him for it.

For the band's entire existence—two and a half years or so—it was perfect, and everything it did was unpredictable and new. All bands of any ambition had to reassess themselves in light of them. I can't deny that they demoralized me some, and I also resented the way they failed to acknowledge how much they'd gotten from New York and me. But in fact what difference would that have made anyway? It doesn't really serve a person to be recognized as an influence on another more popular and successful person. I didn't want that role. I couldn't help being a little jealous of them though. I felt almost as if they were my dream, my mental production—that, as Chris had said, they were four of me.

The Clash were also big. By late 1977, punk had existed to some extent in England for a year and a half or so—since the Pistols' obscure early gigs—and the Clash were the next-best-known of the new bands. Their first album, *The Clash*, had been out for a few months and it had peaked at No. 12 on the British charts.

They were managed by a fashion merchant friend and protégé of Malcolm's named Bernie Rhodes. He made the band's deals and helped keep them in effective outfits.

Their music at this time was highly influenced by the Ramones. Each song was a few simple chords bashed out fast in catchy sequence, gone in two minutes, then another. The vocals were a street-limey nonstop shouted harangue. That singing style, originated by Rotten (though he did it much more sneeringly than Joe Strummer), was the hugely influential signature contribution of the British bands to the punk sound (though there had been unmelodic, sarcastically yelled lyrics at CBGB preceding them, sans the exotic accent).

The trip to England quickly exposed—both to the Voidoids and to me—the extent to which I'd become addicted to drugs. I was horribly junk-sick for nearly all of the tour except the days in London. I hadn't experienced serious withdrawal before and I didn't know how to handle it. I was sleepless, in full-body pain, and sweating and vomiting and spurting diarrhea.

In my continuous illness I'd shop desperately, as we traveled, for a certain vile British cough syrup that had a trace of codeine. It was thick and coarse and brown, and I'd have to drink multiple bottles to get any relief. Sometimes I'd throw up from the taste and consistency before it could kick in.

Our record company was another source of disgust and disappointment. For one thing, they hadn't even managed to get the album released in England in time for the tour. Furthermore, we were on the road for three weeks, a new venue every night, and our transport was a minicar. Not a minibus, but a minicar. There was the driver and a band member, chin on knees, in front, and three more band members shoulder to shoulder in back, with the one in the middle swaying for lack of grip.

I also hated the record company's surprise promotional poster that featured a gigantic photo of my head and torso with the skin colored a flat evil green and the pupils missing from the eyes, like an Alice Cooper shock-rock zombie monster.

At the start of the tour I hung out with Johnny Thunders in London (the Heartbreakers had relocated to England a few months after I left the band). He was living with another Heartbreaker or two in a roomy apartment where the pastimes were doing heroin and watching TV. Sitting around one night, Johnny detailed the most perceptive take on professional rock and roll I'd ever heard. He compared it to prizefighting—young nowhere kids busting their skulls in service to a fantasy of the big-time while businesspeople dole out to them promises and little tokens, raking it in on the youths' showings until the kids fall out, sooner than later, broke and brain-dead, everything burned.

At night in London we'd go out to concerts and clubs. Just before we headed out on the road, Cindy Sin, a nice American girl who was a friend of Johnny's, took me out clubbing. I got drunk instantly, and therefore more reckless. She recommended this Mandrax she had. I'd never heard of it. Later I learned Mandrax is methaqualone, which is the same thing as quaaludes. I hadn't done quaaludes before and I didn't know much about them. I've never much liked tranquilizers. But, as I say, my judgment was not good at the time. As a New York junkie, I also disdained any other way of using than shooting up. To a confirmed junkie the high itself is assumed—it's the rush that counts. Mandrax was a heavy pill that had to be crushed and dissolved if you were dumb and desperate enough to insist on trying to inject it. Cindy had works with her and we went into the women's toilets to get off. She was drunk too, but I let her jockey the needle and she missed my vein, pumping the disgusting sludge into the inert flesh of my left forearm. This created a submerged puddle of painful yellow and blue bruising in the muscle that controlled the hand I used for bass fingering, and it lasted for nearly the whole three weeks of the tour.

We weren't used to deferring to other bands. It didn't help that a big Clash tune then, performed by them nightly, was "I'm So Bored with the USA." On top of that, their touring lives were soft. They rolled in a full-sized tour bus, along with a crew who were also mostly old friends. Ari Up from the Slits was along for most of the ride, as was the

With Robert Quine and Mick Jones backstage, 1977
Voidoids UK tour with the Clash.

British guy with whom I spent the most time and whom I liked most of everyone that I met on the trip—Roadent, a speed-freak roadie pal of the Clash.

I'm not saying they weren't good to us or didn't act friendly and even cultivate our goodwill. They were, and they did. Ivan ended up playing on a record of theirs. They praised our performances, and we all stayed in the same hotels and they came around to our rooms and invited us to theirs. The Clash were good people. But that wasn't my main concern.

In fact, the spirit of the Clash and their whole circle was one of teenage high jinks. It was mysterious and a little intimidating to me. I couldn't relate. My world was heavier and darker. But they behaved, as if it were natural, in a spirit of common cause and almost hippie-like communal goodwill.

The British punk culture also seemed strangely asexual. There were some classic teenage sexpectations among stray members of bands, but for the most part the relations between the boys and the girls seemed infantile, like prepubescent. People kidded and cuddled and might even share beds, but it seemed to be bad form to regard each other as sexual prospects. Johnny Rotten himself was the perfect example of this. As charismatic as he was, as a public figure and an artist (which is really all I knew about him), he never seemed to show any interest in sex, or even to acknowledge it existed. In fact he was married already, to Ari Up's mother, a wealthy heiress fourteen years older than him. Even though I myself had had a sustained relationship with a great person who was much older than me, I could only picture Rotten's counterpart as ancient and motherly, because they were married and because of the asexual vibe of the British punk scene.

Gobbing was at its most extreme then. English punk crowds gave tribute and expressed their excitement at concerts by blowing gobs of snotty saliva as violently as they could at the performers. I always suspected that Patti Smith had something to do with inspiring that, because she used to spit onstage sometimes, and she'd toured England (as had the Ramones). The act of spitting did express something about the attitude of the new bands, and theoretically I kind of liked the idea. It was definitely something that put off grown-ups, and after all it really wasn't any more unsanitary than kissing. However, once you experienced that continuous barrage of saliva onstage, any appreciation of it was lost.

The larger venues of the tour felt from onstage like the familiar cold smelly clubs, but expanded. They were dark and grim, but the band played across a gulf, guarded by security personnel, from the crowd. In the Manchester venue of maybe three thousand capacity, just as we began our set we discovered the microphones were dead. I sang and no sound came out, like that nightmare of trying to scream and being unable. We stopped playing and I yelled an explanation, but the crowd couldn't hear. They began jeering and I got more and more frustrated and angry. I freaked, and as I left the stage, I hurled my guitar. It hit a big security guy in the back. He turned and started towards me. I beat it backstage with the band and locked us in the dressing room, laughing, amazed and nervous, until he would accept my apology without demolishing me.

There was that lowlife journalist with the tour named Julie Burchill, whose writing partner was the equally slimy Tony Parsons. From what I understand she'd snagged Paul Simonon, the bass player for the Clash. I liked Paul, he was a good guy. But Burchill was snidely hostile to me and my band.

We got a mostly enthusiastic (or better) press reception on the tour, but there was usually some member of the British-punk-chauvinist press who'd twist reports about the Voidoids and me into cheap mockery. One of them depicted the Manchester incident as an example of my essential cowardice and fraudulence; another—or maybe the same person—described me as terrorized, like cravenly throwing myself to the boards for safety, by a firecracker that went off at a gig. There was a firecracker thrown on stage in Newcastle; it was silly and got no reaction from us except annoyance.

This segment of the pommy press had jumped onto the bandwagon of British punk as a revolutionary proletariat avant-garde from which they pointed fingers at the "posers." Burchill, prime exemplar, was a self-adoring super-ambitious loudmouth, kind of a Fox News, Murdoch-press type, for that mob. The irony was that those journalists were imitating Patti Smith and me in their outspokenness and criticisms of the world, without even knowing it (having gotten theirs from new-comer Rotten), while doing their best to wither us with their copycat contempt. It was creepy and pathetic, that corps of pettiness grabbing at the chance that ideological "punk" gave them to feel noble while behaving disgustingly—like Communist children reporting their parents to the authorities for criticizing political officials at the dinner table.

The only place on the trip I liked was Scotland—Dundee and Edinburgh and Glasgow. Edinburgh was magic, with its narrow winding river under ancient bridges, castle on a hill in the middle of town, whiskey and huge steaks in centuries-old dining halls, snow-complected girls unable to hide the sudden emotional patches of red on their cheekbones. The punk kids of all those Scots towns were eager and smart and sweet.

Later, as the monotony and discomfort of the tour became more and more horrible, the great Roadent introduced me to his antidote for ennui—self-inflicted cigarette burns. It worked and I still have the cherished mementos on my left forearm.

By the end of the first week of our traveling I'd accepted that I wanted to leave rock and roll. (I was spineless! A fatalistic alienated junkie.) I felt that, once I'd made the album, I'd accomplished what I'd set out to do, and I did not want to grind away in an effort to get the world outside of New York to appreciate us. It was too humiliating and the work was too hard.

My main aim in starting a band had been to have an impact on the world, to make myself heard, and have my perceptions and values and ideas affect things. That had happened, even if it was partially indirect. I believed that my contributions to everything that was going on in music and visuals and temporarily "underground" culture would become more widely known eventually and would continue to grow in influence—that it would "all come out in the wash," as Wylie used to say, and it has.

Back in London, at the end of the tour, we had two concerts that we headlined ourselves, with Siouxsie and the Banshees opening. The venue was a ballroom-style club—an open dance floor under a high stage—with a capacity of four or five hundred, called the Music Machine.

We were relieved to be playing our own date again but were angry about the British tour and everything else in the life of the band. As a result we played some of the most violent, aggressive, fast sets of our lives. For me it was no relief though because I was too distanced and depressed by everything, including myself. The sets came out of furious, single-minded, cold determination, like the finish-line sprint at a marathon. We were as tight as a rubber suit by that point too.

The venue was packed and many of the originators of the new British music scene were there, like Johnny Rotten and Sid Vicious (with Nancy), and the Clash's Mick Jones, along with many journalists. When we finished the final set and didn't come back for an encore, Rotten jumped onstage and exhorted the screaming and applauding crowd to continue cheering until we returned. It was a nice gesture. We eventually encored with a Stones song off *Exile on Main Street*, since British punks purported to despise that band. Backstage afterwards, the first thing Rotten said to me was, "God, you've got a big nose." He's a strange mixture.

Another wayward youth present that night who would eventually become a household name in the UK was Paula Yates. She was seventeen and the greatest-looking thing in the room apart from my shoes. She had short, bleached white-blond hair; fine, narrow features in a broad face, like Demi Moore; and quite large breasts, fully worthy of their braless, near-full visibility through her wispy blouse.

At the time she was working as a "rent-a-punk." She hired out to go to parties to make them look modish. Within a few years she had a rock and roll interview show on British TV's Channel 4. She became big British tabloid fodder and married (Sir) Bob Geldof, pretentious promoter of the Band Aid and Live Aid charities and front man for the cornball Irish "new wave" band Boomtown Rats. In the nineties she had a notorious affair, while still married, with Michael Hutchence, soon-suicided singer for the Australian commercial pop-rock group INXS. In 2000 she died of a drug overdose.

In her autobiography Yates credits me with teaching her about sex. I'll accept that, though the most I can remember is that I had the requisite remote detachment. We were together for the two weeks or so that I hung around London following the tour before returning home. Soon afterwards she got a tattoo of my name on her arm. It depicted a pretty swallow in flight trailing a banner from its beak that read "Hell." But I didn't stay in touch with her. A few months later when Roberta was in London, Paula explained the tattoo to her and Roberta took a picture of her displaying it. Twenty-four years later I used the arm in that picture on the cover of my *Time* CD, without identifying whose it was. Eventually she had the tattoo removed to spare someone else's feelings.

In those final London days post-tour the other person I spent time with was Nick Kent. He was a rock journalist besotted with Keith Richards. He wore eyeliner in imitation of him. He had black hair and a hook nose and receding chin and was skinny and tall. He never changed his black leather pants, even though they had a tear in the crotch his balls hung through. He was a junkie. He'd been one of the first limeys to notice and write about what was going on at CBGB in 1974–75 and I think that's part of what got him in trouble with the British punks. The rest of what got him in trouble was most likely his journalist's certainty that he knew more about what the bands were doing than the bands themselves did. There'd been an incident where Sid Vicious slung a chain at him, causing actual injury. Kent was the closest British equivalent to Lester Bangs in his not-dumb commitment to full-on crude rock and roll, but he was more contrived and self-conscious, with some dubious motives, and he was derivative of Lester. His writing has gotten worse and worse over time, more and more deludedly self-important and blindly, self-aggrandizingly cynical and fake "knowing." He did know where the drugs were though, back then, and he wanted to be with me and so we climbed a bunch of cold London stairwells together.

I should add that, on the whole, all the above said, I've gotten more attention and respect from the British writers and music public than I have from the American. I admired and envied the activist kids who were doing everything that was going on there in the punk era, making it happen. Maybe they were right about Americans being stodgy and self-centered compared to their version of what broke at CBGB, and maybe they were right too that we corrupted them by introducing junk to the British punk world (the Heartbreakers were accused of this).

Those British kids were honest and spontaneous and unpretentious and funny. They aggressively subverted old ideas of what bands were and how they should behave. Most of that came from Malcolm and Rotten, but the kids were so ripe for it that it was theirs too, and they developed it further in fanzines and clothes and ways of life and fresh bands.

Johnny Rotten made everything new by saying things like his band wanted to destroy rock and roll, or that the sacred sixties bands were "old farts." There was a one-for-all, all-for-one feeling among the mass of punk kids there. In America there didn't exist a mass of punk kids, and the few who were conscious of what was happening at CBGB didn't, for the most part, have any ideological or moral or other particular ties with one another. The British kids were all cheeky and mocking, but in a street-smart, kind of lovable and generous way. They took care of each other.

CHAPTER TWENTY-SIX

At the end of 1977 I was approached about playing the lead in a 35 mm color feature film to be called *Blank Generation*, written and directed in New York by a German named Ulli Lommel, about a musician in the CBGB scene. My romantic interest would be the French actress Carole Bouquet.

I thought it might be an alternative to the dead end that music seemed to have become. I didn't know anything about the people involved in the movie, but their credits looked good. Lommel was young, only five years older than me, but he'd been part of the badass German director Rainer Werner Fassbinder's circle in Munich for a decade, mostly as an actor. He'd only recently started directing movies himself but had made two of them. The one he talked about was his latest, *Tenderness of the Wolves*, which had come out in 1973.

His model and mentor Fassbinder was a monster—the apparent successor to Godard in wildly prolific, gorgeous-looking, super-intelligent, politically radical filmmaking. He was also a monster of cocaine-driven tyrannical bitchiness as the boss of his troupe, which otherwise operated like a communal theater company. A given member could act a major role in one movie, production-design another, then assistant-direct, then script-write. But it all had to be at the pleasure of their dictatorial, manipulative leader.

Fassbinder movies are an exotic brew of moody Douglas Sirkian expressionistic high style in dark and spare mise-en-scène, lushly composed and color coordinated; a commitment to radically leftist politics often expressed in the relations of the sexes; and—also Sirkian— overwrought, soap-operatic situations. Gay, cold, and brilliant. He was not in my personal pantheon—the precedence he gave elaborate style wore me out—but he was impressive.

I got the chance to see Lommel's *Tenderness of the Wolves*, and it was pretty inspired—a funny, chilling riff on the story of the real-life serial killer "the Vampire of Düsseldorf," on whom Fritz Lang's 1931 film *M*, with Peter Lorre, was supposed to have been based. The star of *Tenderness*, Kurt Raab, even resembled Lorre, with his moon face, dark eyebrows, and bulging eyes. But in this movie the killer was not only an actual classic super-canine-toothed vampire, he was gay, there was full-frontal nudity of young boys, and he literally butchered them, slicing off cuts that he presented as pork to his grateful neighbors.

Carole Bouquet had been a high-fashion model in France and was only twenty. She spoke English well, but with a strong accent. She'd just begun acting but had played a lead in Buñuel's *That Obscure Object of Desire*. I'd seen that movie, because I tried to see all Buñuel movies. Carole was insanely beautiful, in an inert way. She wasn't dumb, but she wasn't warm. Her beauty almost seemed like a handicap, because it was so extreme that, as she was not particularly animated, it overshadowed any other interesting qualities she might have possessed and made her hard to relate to. She became her beautiful scowling, or insincerely laughing, otherwise inexpressive face.

At first sight, the various connections seemed almost too good to be true, as if the project had condensed from my own history: the despairing but jokey vampire theme of my novelina *The Voidoid*; entan-

With Carole Bouquet in *Blank Generation*
feature fiction film, 1978.

glement with a lovely maddening French soul mate; cinephilia; life in
music (I would be performing some numbers live with the Voidoids at
CBGB) . . .

The band was limping along, essentially on standby. I was demoralized
by the British tour and Sire's sink-or-swim treatment of us, but it was
worse for my bandmates, since my drug addiction and general loss of
initiative were part of the problem for them and now so was my detour
into the movie. I didn't feel responsible to them. I thought the movie
would benefit us, but I didn't consult them before I decided to do it. Of
course, the choice was theirs whether or not to appear in the live music
scenes, but ultimately it was either agree or quit the band.

  We did owe Sire a second album. I had a fantasy that we could do
it as a soundtrack album from the movie, but that didn't make sense,

since the movie's title song came from the first album, and, anyway, I didn't have enough new songs well enough rehearsed to play them in the movie.

I felt fucked over and undervalued by Sire and I didn't want to make another album for them if I could get out of it. I assumed we'd be snapped up by another major label if we were available. I discovered a way in which Sire had violated our contract. They had included on a Sire sampler LP compilation, without informing us, a track, "You Gotta Lose," that we'd recorded during the *Blank* sessions but hadn't used on the album. By contract they were not allowed to do that; they had to have my permission to release anything I hadn't approved for the album. So I figured we could use that violation of theirs to get out of our obligation. Richard Golub got to work on it.

Shooting on the film began in early February 1978. It didn't go as I had hoped. For one thing, I liked hardly anybody who was involved in it.

Lommel turned out to be insufferable. The only artistic qualities he shared with Fassbinder were his megalomania and his bitchiness. I don't thrive in that kind of atmosphere. His dissembling and manipulation and posing were transparent, but somehow a fair number of people enjoyed participating. Maybe their families were like that, so it made them feel comfortable. Anyway, it bored me and I wouldn't play along. But as shooting progressed my disappointment became more and more angry, because Lommel was such a bad artist. It was maddening enough that nothing in the movie made any sense, but it was worse that every moment of it was inappropriate, false, and dead. There wasn't an honest frame in the whole film, including the credits and the fade-outs. It was just a pastiche of half-cooked pretensions, the scenes serving neither plot development nor spectacle nor realities of behavior, but only

The Voidoids performing at CBGB in
Blank Generation film, 1978

derivative *ideas*, and not only were the ideas secondhand, but Lommel
had not understood the originals in the movies of his betters. He only
knew that when Godard or Fassbinder or Antonioni or Warhol had
done the thing (focused on underground and youth culture, or equated
cameras with firearms and/or sex organs, or quoted fifties American
directors) it had made them famous and admired.

Lommel was a hack of the art movie, which is a dizzyingly self-
defeating job description. In the coming years, after another movie
or two in that mode, he found his level and became a hack of horror/
slasher films, which is far more practical. There is an audience for derivative incompetent horror trash, because there's a huge audience for
well-made horror. There is virtually no audience for avant-garde art
movies, so what the fuck could he have been thinking, trying to exploit
it by cheap imitation? Of course the answer is that he didn't know that
Godard and Fassbinder and Antonioni and Warhol actually were bril-

liant and talented (witness the contemptuous way he treats Warhol in *Blank Generation*). He actually thought that everybody was as fake as he himself was.

There was one uniquely good thing about the film: the scenes of the Voidoids playing live at the peak of our best-sounding, best-playing period (with the possible exception of our first few gigs in 1976). The film was shot right after we returned from the Clash tour, and we were tight, and, as it was shot at CBGB, we were in our environment, too. It's not documentation of an actual gig—it's a movie, where the director has contrived the offstage action—but the band is playing exactly as during a gig, and directly into the sound recorder, and the live sound has not been tampered with or added to; it is authentically live playing. Within a few months I'd have abandoned bass and would only grudgingly rehearse and play at all; there would be a different drummer too.

During the period of the movie shoot I had dinner one night with Susan Sontag. The meeting had been arranged by Victor Bockris, Andrew Wylie's old partner, in order to tape the conversation for *Interview* magazine. Bockris had become a prolific journalist specializing in covering William Burroughs and a few other drug-friendly, important, popular hip artists (Keith Richards, Andy Warhol).

I'd long admired Sontag, as did most halfway literate people. She was about twenty years older than me and had been a trendsetter among New York intellectuals all that time. She set the standard for aesthetic and moral values, and for subtlety of perception, in her essays on literature and film (and dance and photography, and a few other art mediums). She affirmed an "erotics" of art rather than an interpretation of it. Furthermore she was beautiful physically and a gracious, charming person.

The dinner was just the three of us, in February, at Bockris's apartment on Perry Street in the West Village. It took place during the final hours of one of the heaviest snowstorms ever recorded in the city. Drifts were fifteen feet high. The snow made everything feel even more rarified and intimate and beautifully insulated. Victor intrepidly fetched Susan from uptown, and Roberta Bayley kept her appointment to show up after dinner to take photos. The shots she got of Sontag and me as pals are some of my favorites of my career.

It bugged me how tolerant Sontag was of Bockris in conversation, and, in retrospect, I'm surprised at how forbearing she was with me, too. Victor was always trying to sound shockingly insightful about modern culture, as if he were Andy Warhol crossed with Marshall McLuhan or something. He also loved to name-drop. But his big pronouncements were clumsily fake and unamusing. ("Unless you have a full-time live-in person, most people don't have the time to get sex," he said that night.) It was instructive, if frustrating, to see how patient (in my view), or routinely respectful (in more neutral terms), Sontag was with him. I wanted her to bond with me.

Still, it was a magical few hours, tucked cozily murmuring and laughing, in that little apartment perched five or six stories up into the whole nighttime city outside hung in glittering white curves, the street surfaces lit in blurry stains by the streetlights and signals and signs, the only sound the clicking of the traffic-light mechanisms, no people anywhere to be seen.

There was one thing she said that I didn't understand at all until many years later. She said that she "hated opinions," that she'd rather not have them. I thought she was being like Victor in contrarian incitement. I took it for granted so completely that opinions defined a person, that one was the sum of one's opinions and that the point was to have interesting ones, that I could only think she meant something else,

With Susan Sontag. *it was a magical few hours*

like "prejudices" rather than opinions. Wasn't her whole identity the opinions she spun out in her essays? No, she meant opinions, and that lately she'd been thinking that she wrote the essays to get rid of them, to make "space for other things." In a way, I was right, because opinions will solidify into prejudices that substitute for perception. Over the years I've finally come to realize that once arrived at, opinions dry up and die, and you have to sweep them away, as she said.

CHAPTER TWENTY-SEVEN

The band had more than enough offers for well-paying gigs. We were popular in New York, and with the ongoing headlines about punk,* there were dozens of nearby dives, not just in New York, but in Philadelphia and New Haven and Pittsburgh and DC and Boston, where we could make decent money. But I usually didn't want to play shows, at least not in a systematic way that would take us up levels. By the end of March, Marc Bell, our drummer, was complaining that he was earning so little that he'd actually had to eat dog food. (We split gig earnings evenly, but I got a bigger share of record royalties—the advance—as well as more money, as main composer, from songwriting and publishing rights than the band.) When the chance came around for him to make a steady paycheck by replacing Tommy Ramone in

---

* For instance, a long feature in *Time* magazine on July 11, 1977, that described "the demon-eyed New Yorker who could become the Mick Jagger of punk, Richard Hell. The music aims for the gut. Even compared with the more elemental stylings of 1950s rock 'n' roll which it closely resembles punk rock is a primal scream. The music comes in fast, short bursts of buzz and blast. Some groups have but two or three chord changes at their disposal, occasionally less: last week at CBGB's a fledgling group set several unofficial records for length of time played without changing chords at all." It also quoted five lines from "Blank Generation," calling it "already a punk classic."

the continuously touring Ramones, he took it. (Tommy disliked going on the road as much as I did.) I didn't even notice that Marc was gone. He was a cheerful funny guy who well held up his end with us while he was there, but he probably fit better with the Ramones, where he could work in a system and also get the ego gratification of serving not just as drummer but in a band that presented its members as "brudders."

At about the same time I decided to stop playing bass. It's limiting and difficult to play bass while singing. The bass has to keep a strict rhythm, while the vocal is better if it slides around in the beat unpredictably. Bass players who sing, like Paul McCartney or Sting, usually write songs in a style that allows them to match a rhythmically consistent vocal with a simple bass line. I wanted to experiment more with my vocal phrasing, and I knew my bass playing was inferior anyway.

Quine hated me quitting bass. He thought my bass playing was valuable. I am a rotten bass player but I think I know what he meant. The more competent musicians we got to play bass didn't sound as good as I did. They were smooth, but our repertoire worked, when it did, partly because it was all a little off-kilter. The performances and arrangements catch you unexpectedly. There's an unusual liveliness to it. It kind of requires that you pay attention and listen to it on its own terms, but if you're willing to do that it can blow your mind. If you're not willing it can sound pathetic, but so be it. Mere competence is always boring.

We'd succeeded in breaking off our commitment to Sire, and we had people looking at us. Earl McGrath, the head of Rolling Stones Records, began coming to gigs and he told us that Mick was seriously considering signing us, though I don't remember ever hearing that a Rolling Stone was at a show. It didn't get further than that. Private

Stock, Blondie's original label, did make an offer, but we didn't think it was acceptable. That company seemed to be failing anyway.

Then Jake Riviera started talking to me about where I was going in music. He'd become very successful as a manager of the Stiff Records early-punk and pub-rock groups. (Pub rock was a fifties-style raucous but catchy British rock and roll genre, associated with gigging in pubs, that just preceded or overlapped punk. Bands that Jake signed to Stiff or managed or both included Nick Lowe, Ian Dury, Elvis Costello, Wreckless Eric, and the Damned.) Jake came from the streets and he looked like it and acted like it. He was stocky and pugnacious—he'd been a boxer who'd considered going professional—and he dressed quasi-rockabilly, in narrow-lapelled sports jackets, thin ties, pointed shoes, and a greasy ducktail. His head was block shaped but his face was open. He wielded aggression in unexpected ways. That was natural to him, but I think he also kind of played it up, and played it warped, partly from a feeling of rivalry with Malcolm McLaren. Malcolm was a genius at unconventional ways of doing things that fostered exactly the right kind of attention for his bands.* Jake pulled numbers too but his pranks and acts of defiance were dubiously random compared to

---

* Like refraining from using the Sex Pistols' priceless appearance on their packaging, but instead using Jamie Reid's graphical equivalent of it, such as Queen Elizabeth with a safety pin through her nose, or the album that had nothing on its cover but the Day-Glo ransom-note paste-up "NEVER MIND THE BOLLOCKS HERE'S THE Sex PisTOLs." These were brilliant ways of keeping faith with the band's insistence that they wanted to destroy rock-god worship, that what they did was what anybody could do, and was done by everybody for everybody. Or how he had them play an earsplitting set on a houseboat floating down the middle of the Thames on the queen's jubilee. Or how on their American tour, they skipped the Northeast and L.A. to play most of their shows in the backwater working-class South.

Malcolm's.* Probably what Jake was best at was intimidating people. He liked to be a loose cannon in his dealings with the record industry and it could be effective. He was like Bogart in *The Maltese Falcon* flipping out at Sydney Greenstreet and company, breaking glass and screaming and threatening, but as soon as he shuts the door behind him, grinning gleefully, and then grinning again to see the adrenaline still making his hand tremble.

Jake was a stand-up guy for me, including materially, helping me out when I needed it; he didn't just try to make money off me.** He wanted to bring out our second album. He had a new label, having moved on from Stiff, that he called Radar. The plan was that we'd record a single that year, 1978, with Nick Lowe producing, and then in December and January tour England for three weeks opening for Costello, and after we returned we'd prepare to make an album. Jake/Radar would pay for all this.

That was something we agreed on in early fall. In the meantime, the spring and summer following the movie shoot, the band was staggering along, playing when I reckoned necessary, teaching songs to bass player Jerry Antonius and drummer Frank Mauro, and annoying each other.

---

* For example, the way he had numbered with "#0001" a large batch of the limited number-stamped five-thousand-copy 1976 "Blank Generation" single on his Stiff Records, as well as a set of copies that were numbered above five thousand.

** Malcolm was like this with musicians too, and so was Hilly, for that matter. These three were the successful music-business people I dealt with who were actually sympathetic with the bands and generous and loyal towards them, not just exploitive. It wasn't like the relationships I had with other music-business people, like Seymour or Gottehrer or Thau, who saw me only as something from which they might be able to profit a little.

To be explicit, the real constant for me, the headquarters, the center from which all other paths radiated like a world-sized cobweb, during those years, was my opiated solitude. It seemed as worthy a way of being as another, metaphysically. I was still myself inside the drugs, and I was reasonably true to my values, such as they were. The condition just got boring eventually, and, while "victimless" in ways, it could be dangerous to those nearby who didn't understand about the egocentricity of it. Most of my life was interior, possibly by that token empty, which may be another way of saying metaphysically faithful.

On the bright side, life was interesting (that subcategory of boring) on drugs, and in a way more pure and direct than without. I didn't conceal anything or accept any nonsense (except my own). A person actually has fewer problems when addicted, too, in that any problems are subsumed into the supreme problem of getting enough drugs not to be sick that day. It was also interesting to scientifically manipulate one's consciousness and pleasure centers and energy level the way the drugs allowed.

Addiction followed from who and where I was. There's no disentangling the qualities that led me to use drugs from those that led to more acceptably positive achievements. I wrote "Blank Generation" and conceived Theresa Stern and her views and attitudes, and wrote *The Voidoid,* which are of consummate junkie mentality, before any real narcotics use. It was my natural state, the druggy psychology. I have many fond memories of the narcotics life. There's an extreme intensity to it that, like being in combat, can't be understood except by those who have undergone it. I wouldn't wish addiction on anyone, but there's something glorious about it, in a sad way.

Addiction is lonely. It starts as pure pleasure, and the degeneration, in a few quick years, into a form of monumental compulsive-obsessive condition is actually more psychological than physical. Once the drug use has replaced everything else, life becomes purely a lie, since in order to keep any self-respect, the junkie has to delude himself that use is by choice. That's the worst loneliness—the isolation, even from oneself, in that lie. In the meantime the original physical pleasure becomes merely dull relief from the threat of withdrawal, from the horror of real life. The user will add any other drugs available, especially stimulants, like methedrine or cocaine, to try to make it interesting again. Eventually, I happened to survive using long enough to reach a place where I couldn't kid myself anymore that it was all on purpose, and the despair and the physical torment of my failed attempts to stop became my entire reality. I found a way to quit, with help. It was luck that I lived that long.

Addiction does have an effect on an addict's work. It reduces production and increases self-indulgence. A narcotics addict doesn't demand as much of himself as he would if he were straight. If an addicted artist is very, very good, a reasonable amount of interesting work can be done, but it will probably be fragmentary and rambling, and chances are there will be far more unrealized or abandoned projects than there would have been otherwise.

I realize that this description of addiction is self-contradictory in its mix of affirmation, resigned acceptance, and rejection of narcotics use, but still it is true.

Already, in 1978, I'd learned and recognized enough of this about my addiction that I spent most of that summer enduring endless suffering in attempts to kick. It was thankless too, in the sense that, as a junkie, I couldn't expect any sympathy. I did have the blessings and care of one stupendously generous person, Susan Springfield (once and future name: Susan Beschta), who was my girlfriend for a year or so around this time. She was the front person for a band of three girls and one guy called the Erasers. The band never found a real identity outside of their inspired name, but they were all good people. Jody Beach, their bass player, ended up marrying ace British session guitarist Chris Spedding. Their drummer was called Jane Fire. For a while, the artist and art writer David Ebony played keyboards for the band, and for a while Richie Lure, Heartbreaker Walter's fresh-faced younger brother, played guitar.

When I first started seeing Susan, earlier in that year, the three girls in the band shared a loft, where they also rehearsed, on Elizabeth Street just below Houston. They threw great parties there. At one of them Iggy Pop requisitioned their gear and recruited a couple of guitar players from the partiers and sang and writhed for everybody. Rotten came around a few times when he was in New York, just after the Pistols had disintegrated.

I had an unprecedented experience there one morning when I woke up on a mattress on the floor, after a long strenuous night, with the course of an entire complex story in my head, carried back from unconsciousness. It depicted how some members of the most neglected, despised class of citizen—being a group of friends who are as socially handicapped and downright (mildly) dislikable as their file-clerk- and bank-teller-type jobs are boring—become, in the course of a dramatic and gruesome narrative, heroes. I published an awkward, sloppy version of the plotline in the *East Village Eye* as "Lowest Common Dominator" (which title I later used for an unrelated song about Ulli Lommel). It was an awesome experience to have every detail of an entire feature film or pulp fiction story appear in my head fully formed.

I made another crude and virtually unknown New York movie in 1978 too, a faux-noir feature called *Final Reward*. It was largely copped, I eventually realized, from Jules Dassin's 1955 masterpiece of a dark heist flick, *Rififi*, but was shot for almost nothing in 16 mm black and white.

I think I was the only actor in it who was paid. The director, Rachid Kerdouche, thought I was the blank Mickey Rourke, art-slum music's romantic tortured embodiment of coolness. (All my career I've been described as quintessentially "cool" or "hip." I suppose I've fostered this, on levels, in order to seem desirable to girls and to avoid standard hypocrisy and routine consumer life, but I am not cool. I'm cranky under pressure, I'm a mediocre athlete, I get obsessed with women, I usually want to be liked, and I'm not especially street-smart.) Rachid's view of me was flattering, all things considered, but I wouldn't have made the movie if he hadn't paid me the $50 a day or whatever it was I needed to maintain my drug habit. My acting in it was even worse than in Lommel's flick, mostly because my degeneration had had a few more months to progress since then.

I hadn't met Rachid until he contacted me about the acting job (it had nothing to do with my job for Lommel because that movie wasn't edited until 1979). He was the son of North African Berber nomads who'd immigrated to France for work. His father became a miner, but Rachid thought about nothing but movies, genre movies—Sam Peckinpah and John Huston and Howard Hawks and Robert Aldrich—and had found his way to New York. He was about my age and wore flecked and stained black sports jackets and scuffed black pants and shoes and was fleshy and dark haired and smiled a lot. His abiding treatment of everyone affectionately kiddingly could seem overly familiar, but he was a sweet guy.

The script was nuts, but theoretically he had a cast that could make it work. Everyone had been recruited from the underground night-life of late-seventies New York. Teri Toye, who was a male-to-female transsexual—later an inspiration and runway model for Stephen Sprouse—played a shady nightclub owner, Sam(antha), who, in a nice double reverse, is supposed to be a woman posing as a man. Sam's doofus strong-arm stooges were played by Geoffrey Carey (who ended up in Paris—I noticed him in the Arnaud Desplechin movie *Kings and Queen* a few years ago) and platinum-blond real-life go-go boy John Sex. The princely, suave, veteran East Village painter Bill Rice played a corrupt police detective. I had the lead role of a guy just released from prison who was the king of the New York demimonde but now has rivals. He decides to pull a complex heist largely to help his burned-out former gang "feel alive" again. John Heys, noted for his wicked Diana Vreeland looks and protruding ears, from the Ridiculous Theatrical Company, was one of my criminal crew, and, most consequentially, Cookie Mueller played my wandering girlfriend.

Cookie became one of my best friends for the coming two or three years and really never stopped being that, though we saw less of each other later. As an actress, she was known for the scene in *Pink Flamingos* in which John Waters had gotten her to try to have sex with a chicken. Eventually she became a downtown health advice columnist for the *East Village Eye*. Those two sentences go well together. She would also become an inspired art critic for *Details*, and a kick-ass memoirist, and the archetypical subject of the photographs that made Nan Goldin famous.

She came from Baltimore, "the hairdo capital of the world," which is how she ended up acting for Waters. She was a trailer-park-style girl. When I met her, she was go-go dancing, freelance, for an agency. She always recommended go-go dancing for its healthful and cosmetically beneficial properties. She did have the most muscular ass of any woman I've ever known. Her closest friend was her longtime lover, named Sharon Niesp, a white girl from Baltimore too, who had an amazing gospel voice and would eventually hook up with the Neville Brothers' Ivan Neville in New Orleans, but everybody loved Cookie, because she was all heart.

She came from Baltimore

Cookie had an unusually large railroad apartment on Bleecker Street, just east of Seventh Avenue. Sixties girl-group music (Chiffons, Shangri-Las) was always yearning and berating in harmony there among the kitschy and quasimorbid curiosity-cabinet contents of her cozy bad-girl crib. It was the perfect place to rest your head in highness. Once the New York painting scene started taking off in the early eighties and she started writing her art column for *Details*, she benefited from many wack neo-expressionist and graffiti paintings that suited her digs perfectly, too, bestowed by admiring young artists. She shared the apartment with her small son, Max, whose father was in some other city.

Cookie was nonjudgmental. She had a lot of respect for criminals. She understood why everybody did everything, but she was no kind of earth mother. Cookie wasn't serene or self-confident. She was serious about her appearance but was hardly ever satisfied with it. Her ideal in that line was a personalized, thrift-store version of girl-group styles of big hair, a lot of black and blue eye makeup, glossy lipstick, short and tight skirts, and spike heels. She was great at doing her look, but it could take her hours to work up the exact ensemble in which she was willing to go public.

It's easy to see why she was Nan Goldin's muse. Nan lived and worked in the gay and wild-kids' art gutter, and Cookie was the biggest-hearted, funniest citizen of it, as well as way photogenic. She had an unusual face. Her superhero jaw and thinnish lips made her look almost transvestite, especially when she was fully made up. She had bee-stung eyelids; a crisp, small nose; and hair voluptuously long and thick and always dyed, usually frosted and streaked. When she smiled, her lips flattened into wide brush marks too, like some goddess of joy, Marilyn Monroe. She didn't hold anything back, and she loved to laugh, and her nose would stretch and flatten, Genghis Khan–Marlene Dietrich style, when she did, and her hooded eyes would scrunch completely shut, her head thrown back, laughing full throated, like a schoolgirl, no hardness at all.

My favorite fairy tale has always been "Hansel and Gretel." It has everything. I've always liked being with a sister sans supervision— lost—and I like cake too, and self-reliance and ingenuity. But, strangely, considering that the refuge in "Hansel and Gretel" is really a death trap, the most magical thing about the story is the way it nevertheless evokes a glowing warm haven deep inside the ominous cold forest. And that's what Cookie's apartment was like, and it was made of Cookie!

Furthermore, she had cocaine. Well, that was a little later. But she did end up dealing cocaine and ecstasy and even heroin, to supplement her single-ma food stamps. She used the drugs herself too, but she was good at keeping to her self-imposed consumption limits. (A line of hers to me: "Your capacity for overindulgence is bigger than mine.")

She called everybody "hon," as in "honey." Her skin was honey, her hair was honey, her writing was honey. The smartest, most bitchy people, like Rene Ricard and Gary Indiana, loved her because she was purely goodwilled, quick, and nurturing, and she reveled in trashiness, her own and others', and the throwaway low bon mot (which talent she eventually turned into her memoiristic literature). She was game for anything. I don't know much about her lesbian relationships, but I know she loved having sex with men and didn't hesitate when opportunities of any interest arose. I didn't know her in love. We would do drugs and have sex and laugh and talk. I understand one of her most intense, obsessed New York affairs was with a man who perpetrated very rough sex. She was said to love him. She eventually married a wonderful, sweet, perfect Cookie-partner of an excitable, mystical, extremely handsome Italian artiste named Vittorio, and they accepted heroin addiction together.

That fall—on Saturday, October 28, 1978—we played a show at CBGB that was important because it was broadcast live on the radio (WPIX) and was so well recorded that most of it ended up getting released, much later (in 2002), on my CD *Time* (which also included the London Music Machine gig). The date showed what we were like back in the USA (glad to be home), with a new bass player and drummer. It was a benefit for St. Mark's Church, arranged by its tenant the Poetry Project, to raise money for restoring the church after a terrible fire, and there were a lot of poets there, along with the CBGB mob.

Elvis Costello, with whom we were due to tour England soon, was in town and he asked to join us for a song or two. I sang a new number, "The Kid with the Replaceable Head," even though I'd only written two of the three verses. I just repeated the second verse. When we brought Elvis on, he said I should be president. Then he sang my song "You Gotta Lose." For the finale, in honor of the church, we did a surprisingly skillful version of the Stones' "Shattered." Allen Ginsberg and Ted Berrigan were in the crowd. I secretly kidded them in my patter, with an "om" dropped in for Allen, and then, to blow Ted's mind, since he had no reason to think I'd ever heard of him, an unacknowledged paraphrase of a few lines of his—appropriated, as if they were mine, the way he would do. He was always really nice to me afterwards.

In late October we recorded the "Kid with the Replaceable Head" single (backed with "I'm Your Man") with Nick Lowe producing, for Jake's Radar Records. I thought I was making a pop hit with "Kid." I even diluted the lyrics in the chorus because I thought they might be too morbid for the public. (The original chorus went, "Look out! Here he comes again. / They say he's dead. He's my three best friends. / He's so honest that the dishonest dread / meeting the kid with the replaceable head." I changed "dead" to "done" on the single.) On December 15 we left for London, where we would do a few Christmas shows with Elvis before the three-week British tour with him.

True to my pattern, I actually believed I was clean when I left. My test was whether I could go three days without heroin or methadone.

Inevitably, after confirming that way my freedom from addiction, I'd celebrate by getting high on the fourth day (or the end of the third).

Jake did a creative thing for us in London by renting a houseboat on the Thames, off Cheyne Walk, for the band to live in. But it turned out not to be a good idea to cram us all into a tight space. By the end of the first three days I was junk-sick and irritable. Quine was always impatient and grouchy on tour. The weather got cold, and not only was the boat underheated, but heavy snowfall upriver raised the water level so much that the gangway to the dock got submerged and for a while we were stranded offshore. I shivered and sweated in my clammy bedclothes, trying not to count the minutes in my cold sleeping cabinet as I read, randomly, C. S. Lewis's *Voyage to Venus*. I copied a line from it into my notebook, "that terrible power which the face of a corpse sometimes has of simply rebuffing every conceivable human attitude one can adopt towards it." I knew about Lewis's Christian agenda in his fantasy/science fiction and it cheapened him for me, but I've stolen the concept of that line a few times over the years.

My hopelessness grew. I gave an interview to a major music paper in London where I said that my ideal existence would be to have an intravenous drip of heroin while getting a blow job, with some oatmeal on the side for health purposes. ("See, for me, every kinda effort seems a compromise.")

Quine got fed up with me. The whole past year's disappointments for which I was responsible now had the pressures of touring added. For the first time he lost his temper. On top of my faithlessness in doing the flick and refusing to gig much, the problem of my quitting bass had been compounded by our having signed on an impossible freak to replace me. He was a young guy, not dumb, but seemingly devoid of character except for the determination to be consistent with Bob and me. He was like a sociopath; all his powers of perception were focused on compiling analyses of what we said and did, to be employed in the creation of algorithms intended to generate behavior by him consistent with ours. It was pathetic and repulsive, and it made me feel like a parody myself. I was walking around with a mean-spirited caricature as a shadow. He was really the "blank" one. I was a fraud who pretended to blankness. It got labyrinthetically self-repellant.

The entire Costello tour was just a stretched-out version of those first few cold, angry, nauseated days on the houseboat.

CHAPTER TWENTY-EIGHT

A round 1979, things start to become a blur, not because they moved fast or because I can't remember them but because of the way everything got absorbed into the drug monotony. It was like my real human life was a thin network on a sticky medium of drug routine that for the next five or six years rolled around in my limited environments every day into a smeared filthy wadded sphere of undifferentiated drug dimness, the little veins of any real pure life lost and dirtied inside. Hopelessness, depravity, and fun.

After I took the money Jake had given me to make demos for the album he wanted, I recorded him only four new songs, which, along with other evidence of my useless condition, led him to indefinitely postpone the album we'd planned.

I had a booking agent who indulged me, a nice guy who was in too deep, named Robert Singerman. I could always get him to take care of me. I let my band disintegrate and would just rehearse whomever I could muster when times got desperate enough that I'd commit to a cheap Singerman tour.

I started contributing a column, "Slum Journal," to the new monthly *East Village Eye*. I got a hundred dollars per tabloid page of each installment, I was guaranteed a minimum of a full page an issue, and I was allowed to publish whatever I wanted. The writing was usually atrocious because I didn't meaningfully care and I was overdoing stimulants.

The coke and speed I'd started relying on to counteract the narcosis acted as aphrodisiacs, not that I needed much intensification in that area. Cocaine itself is like an orgasm shuddering the nervous system for ten or twenty minutes. (Heroin is like sex too, but the postcoital swoon.) It's funny how, being as coke is like sex itself, it increases the desire—and ability—to seduce partners for actual sex as well. I guess it's like it takes money to make money. And, like money too, no amount is enough. When coke is injected, rather than snorted, the crash is especially bad because a shot starts the high at peak. To maintain, I had to shoot up every fifteen minutes. Thirty years later, I still have the scars on my left forearm. At the time they were a crusty thick twine of scab from the inside of my elbow to my wrist.

Under coke my brain and cock were one. Alone at three AM in my dingy apartment, I would phone some girl the look in whose eyes I'd noticed that week and ask her to come over and let me close-up draw her naked between-legs. She would always agree, for two reasons: my powers of persuasion, and I knew how to pick them. Plus I had cocaine. We'd do a couple of doses and she'd undress and lie on her back on my mattress and I'd stretch out between her thighs with a pad and pencil. Many do secretly love to be released from sentiment or initiative into submission to a trusted other's ultra-deliberate sexual orchestration. It's like drifting on a warm current in the moonlight, with lots of shooting stars, and kisses from the fishies, an occasional muscular tentacle entering, or maybe a little electrified eel.

Sex pervades all, so it would seem necessary to treat it in the description of anyone, but it's hard to describe one's own sex experience well because people—any audience—have so much of their self-image and self-esteem wrapped up in sex. Everyone's sensitive to how it's talked about, including me, because, again, bodies are wired to want overwhelmingly to reproduce themselves (have sex), and that depends on one's sex appeal. Anything said about sex is going to push people's buttons and arouse resentments, interfering with communication. So maybe I should stick to masturbation here. That's less threatening, anyway. Often enough, on those solitary cocaine nights I'd opt to masturbate rather than invite over a girl, since, no matter what, another's presence complicates things. I'd get my sketch pad and number 2 pencil and take off my clothes and sit down in front of a full-length mirror in my derelict bedroom and draw my cock to orgasm. My incest fantasies were about having sex with myself. It seemed self-evidently the erotic pinnacle. Self-evidently. After all, who knows better what one likes than oneself?

I wasn't all that sophisticated. I had my first genuine experience of sadomasochistic or dominant-submissive sex that year too. There had been the time when I'd been in Television and I had a little reunion with Ruth Kligman (who was notorious as the ingenue Elizabeth Taylor–lookalike art groupie who'd been with her lover Jackson Pollock in the car when he crashed to death—she later had affairs with de Kooning and even Jasper Johns). One drunken drug-sodden night I let Richard Lloyd tag along to her loft with me and she was excited to have us tie her to her bed in her underwear, etc. But that was comparatively slight as S & M.

My introduction to the real, complex pleasures of slave ownership began on a hot summer night in 1979, at the loft of my crystal meth dealer. He cultivated relationships with people who had nightlife reputations. Usually I would do a line, cop mine, and split. That night I lingered because his girlfriend wandered into my range further than she had before and I really noticed her. She was a tall blonde, quite young, with thick, straight, shoulder-length hair, a curvaceous figure, and a broad-featured but beautifully proportioned, prepubescently complected face, Kate Winslet style. She was barefoot and wore well-cut leg-hugging creased white slacks and a long-sleeved blue and white striped shirt, like a French sailor. We kidded each other a little bit. Another customer arrived and the girlfriend and I drifted into a corner, talking. She was a student at the Fashion Institute of Technology. She'd designed and sewn the pants she was wearing.

The dealer soon told me that they were about to go to a nearby club to see a band and asked if I'd like to come along. In the dark club, one of the things his girl shyly confided into my ear was that she always wanted to completely lose herself in sex. Her boyfriend decided he had to retrieve a tape recorder from the loft. Still, she resisted going home with me. I said he'd accepted our situation or he wouldn't have left the way he did. Look how long he was taking, too. We'd already kissed. She relented.

Back at my apartment we were both most of the way undressed in the quick but unhurried distance from the front door to the bedroom. Near-naked, sitting facing each other on the bed in the moonlight, her breasts gleaming, she told me something that I hadn't realized she'd meant when she'd said she liked to lose herself. She wanted me to take control of her. I owned her and she wanted me to use her.

As I slapped her, it dawned on me that there was more to it than I'd realized, that what she'd said had made me her slave. It had made her my ideal, but that was to enslave me, as a writer is slave to his "muse." It was like she was a language in sex that I would use to write a poem. But I had to use her in the way that excited her, or the work would be a failure. (Of course I could just have gone crude and treated her as sub-human, disregarding her actual responses, and in fact I did do versions of that, but consciously, with deliberation, and for her sake as much as mine. It was complicated.)

I was inspired by the desire to please her by exercising her slavery as fully as possible! I wanted to ravish and dominate her beyond anything that had ever occurred to her could be, and to fully employ my faculties in the game.

She left at dawn. I was high from the experience for days, for long after the drugs wore off. I assumed that it would change my future love life. It didn't really. There've been a few incidents and relationships, but I'm too lazy to be a committed dominator, too relaxed and eclectic. Being a slave owner is hard work. That's the beauty and the reward of it, but still . . . Some years later when Kathy Acker wanted me to slap her while I fucked her in the ass, it was hard to work up the motivation, even to keep a straight face. Not that I didn't enjoy it.

In 1980 I carried out Jake Riviera's lavish commission to leisurely drive a sky-blue 1959 Cadillac across America. Jake collected cars and had found the Cadillac on the West Coast. The '59 was the model with the most exaggerated fins of all the rocket cars of the fifties. The legend was that a bike rider had been fatally impaled on one. Roberta Bayley and I were to pick it up from a mechanic in Venice, California, and drive it back to New York. Jake would cover all the expenses and we could design any route and take as long as we wanted on the road. Roberta's job was to take photographs along the way, and mine was to take notes, with the idea of making a big book from the trip, a kind of punk chronicle of the USA. As it turned out, the drive was a drug-sick, broke-down farce and disaster, and a worse problem was that I was too chemically oppressed to write much of anything afterwards. (Instead, nearly fifteen years later the assignment became the premise for *Go Now*.)

The following year I acted in the movie *Smithereens,* directed by Susan Seidelman. I had my methadone from Fernando and I kept it to a minimum, so for practical purposes I was competent and reliable (with a few blips). Still, I existed in a whole other realm from Susan and her NYU filmmaking crew. They were straight. Susan was a bit nervous about my level of responsibility so she invited me to stay with her while we were shooting and I agreed. It was cozy at her apartment: good food, goodwill, and specialized VIP treatment.

Smithereens is by far the best film I've been a part of. It was the story of a girl on the outskirts of the "new wave" music scene in New York who wanted to be famous despite lacking any particular talent. I played a hustling musician she saw as her ticket to the top. The script was the first one by Ron Nyswaner, who would write the Academy Award–winning *Philadelphia* a few years later. Seidelman's follow-up effort was *Desperately Seeking Susan. Smithereens* had a lot of charm if it wasn't exactly aesthetically exciting. It was a kind of liberal Hollywood mixture of sympathy and cynicism in its conception of the New York quasipunk club scene of the time.

I liked the people on the production. Susan Berman, who played the lead, Wren, was a darling even if she wouldn't really kiss me. I got most close to a guy on the crew, the camera operator, Ken Kelsch. He'd been a Green Beret in Vietnam and was still scrambled from that experience. We'd stay up drinking and talking.

(I'd been interested in the Vietnam War for a while, for everything it revealed about the state of things. I thought that the best books to come out of that war made up a lot of the best American writing of the second half of the century, and I collected rare editions of them: Michael Herr's *Dispatches,* Tim O'Brien's *The Things They Carried,* Philip Caputo's *A Rumor of War,* Gustav Hasford's *The Short-Timers,* etc. The books not only dealt with essential matters of life, but, I eventually realized, they also served as antidotes to self-pity for me. Things could be much worse! I also collected books about concentration camp life for the same reasons, I think.)

Filmmaking as a profession is unique, short of life-threatening, for its emotional intensity. Everyone is so raw, as artists under pressure—to justify the huge money investment and deal with unforeseeable new crises every day—and everyone involved is so dependent on each other to make it all work, it becomes like a crazed, devoted family. And then suddenly it's finished and everyone parts, and the whole process is undertaken again with a different set of people in whole other roles, somewhere else. For the actors it's especially insane—they have the relationships with each other their roles demand, on top of whatever "real" relationships with each other they may have (and, as a rule, they are magnetic beings); they have to be prepared all day to immediately shed any inhibitions and produce specialized, assigned behavior that looks natural and spontaneous despite bright lights and all the strange human attention focused on them; they need pampering to be in the best position to focus on behaving in those unlikely ways, while at the same time they've got to maintain the sympathy of everyone on the set because the success of the project depends on everyone's mutual help . . . It's hard work. Actors really do earn their big paychecks.

That year my girlfriend was a coke dealer named Anne. She'd recently come to New York from San Francisco, where she'd been working as an escort. She was smart and talented—a lighting designer for theater—but insecure (she's since become very successful in her field and overcome that insecurity). She was stick-skinny, though she had a perfectly ample ass, and her breasts were minuscule and she was embarrassed and self-conscious about that. She'd been insulted by clients for it. Her face was pixie and very pale and looked especially ivory against her shiny-black hair. I wrote odes to her breasts, which were essentially slightly swollen nipples. I did like them because they were novel and perverse (for their resemblance to children's or boys'). She permitted me huge quantities of coke. We fucked frenziedly all over her carpeted studio, and then in emergencies I would crawl around the floor, spastically, my nervous system jerking back and forth in the scary gap between one and zero, trying to identify any little white specks as stray flecks of coke.

That relationship coincided with the recording of my second album, *Destiny Street,* mostly in early 1981, right after I'd shot *Smithereens.* Marty Thau—the guy who'd originally worked with Richard Gottehrer to sign me to the production deal that'd resulted in the *Blank Generation* album—had wangled some money from a small New Jersey distributor called Jem, which operated a record label called Passport, to cheaply record two or three groups' albums. Marty called his company Red Star. Once again I was a sucker—ignorant and naïve regarding the record business. Thau himself was making very little investment but he'd be entitled to approximately 50 percent of earnings.

When I asked Quine to join me, he committed immediately and I took his suggestions for drummer and second guitar, respectively Fred Maher and Naux (pronounced Naw-OOSH—originally Juan Maciel). I didn't consider Ivan from the original Voidoids because I wanted to hear a new guitar combination. We booked two or three weeks' rehearsal time in a studio called 171A, around the corner from me. I felt so dependent on cocaine that I'd bring a syringe and a stash to rehearsal and then excuse myself to go to the bathroom every twenty minutes. I thought the band would accept my explanation that I'd been drinking too much coffee. One afternoon when Bob used the bathroom immediately after me he returned scowling and seething, but still it didn't hit me for another couple of hours that he had to have seen my blood spattered across the porcelain.

Once we started recording, at Intergalactic Studio on the Upper East Side, things broke down further. I couldn't abide Thau and I felt guilty towards the band because of how I'd failed to prepare. I had three or four of the songs only half-arranged: I'd left the proportions of parts to parts (verse, intro, chorus, outro, etc.) undeveloped, and I had no final bass part ready for two or three others. And this was out of a total of seven original songs. Three more cuts were cover versions. I'd also intended to show off my development as a composer by including bridge parts (that single-verse break, like a tune within the tune, that livens up most great songs), but I never got around to it.

Amiable Alan Betrock was producer of the album. As the proprietor of tiny Shake Records, he'd released, in 1980, an "extended play" 45 of two of the three of my Neon Boys tunes that we'd recorded in 1973, backed with two recent Voidoids demos (from the sessions Jake had commissioned). Alan wasn't experienced but he was inexpensive, he knew pop music, and he loved my band and me. He was a record collecting fanatical aficionado of sixties pop culture and trash music who'd created the collector-catalog fanzine *Rock Marketplace* in the early seventies, and then founded *New York Rocker* in 1975 when he got excited about the scene at CBGB.

We had about three weeks to record and mix the album and I was too fragile to come into the studio for one of those weeks. I was strung so tightly by cocaine into supersensitivity and paranoia that I couldn't tolerate the thought of stepping outside. If I'd gone into the street, some passing stranger might have unexpectedly coughed in my vicinity and blown me out of my skin. I'd call the studio and try to act as if it was an aesthetic choice to instruct Bob and Naux to add some more guitar in this place or that. As a result, by the time I could summon the strength to return, the record was a piercing, percolating drone of trebly guitar noise.

Then I started singing. The vocals were my last good chance to redeem the record, to make it stand out. God knows I was emotionally exposed. I'd have them turn the studio lights down and I'd stand there alone in the cluttered recording room desperately reaching with everything I had. The Them tune "I Can Only Give You Everything" was harrowing and it stretched through a long rotating outro, over which I laid pained wailing. By the time I got to the end I was in tears. I picked up something and threw it. The recording engineer wanted to indicate his full empathy and participation so he jumped out of his chair at the console, whipped through the door to the studio, and started kicking over the equipment himself, as if it were a celebration.

Despite all this, I did then and do now consider the material on *Destiny Street* to be superior to the set on *Blank Generation*. I'd learned a lot about making songs since 1977. The songs on *Destiny Street* had an internal consistency to them, a more satisfying feeling of inevitability. On the other hand, the songs weren't as unusual in either their style or subjects as the songs on *Blank Generation*, and their arrangements were sloppier. But strictly as a collection of songs, as opposed to performances, *Destiny Street* is the better album.

I was proud of the recording when it got released, but it didn't take long for it to pitch me into despair. All I could hear was my indifference and self-destruction, fatalism and raw mania. It's only in the last few years, a quarter century later, that I find myself respecting the re-

Destiny Street Voidoids play the Peppermint Lounge, 1982
(sax player unidentified).

cord again. The best music writers gave it high marks at the time, but I figured that was just because they were predisposed to favor noise, intellect, and failure. Robert Palmer, the devoted and discriminating music critic for the *New York Times,* named it (in the *Times*) one of the ten best records of 1982 and wrote in *Penthouse,* "Richard Hell and the Voidoids have made the most passionate and vital rock album of the year." Quine brought the first test pressing to Lester Bangs in what turned out to be the week before Bangs died, and Lester told Bob that we'd pulled it off—a worthy successor to *Blank,* which was high praise considering Lester's opinion of the first album. Of course there was no chance whatsoever that it would be a hit seller. Not only was the sound too crazed, but the label was obscure and spottily distributed.

Liva, who was my girlfriend in 1982, was a Dutch vagabond with a mental age of about nine, temporarily working as a call girl. She had a gold tooth, cheerful attitude, and luscious luscious large snow-white tits and blond pubic hair. She'd found her way from Holland to New York City via Borneo aboard cargo ships. If Cookie was honey, Liva was gold—her front tooth, her glinting nakedness in my sunny living room, her lack of interest in making moral judgments, her generosity and happy disposition.

I met her when I woke up in bed with her and another girl from her escort service, in October 1981. We'd spent the night in the sumptuous apartment of one of their clients who'd allowed them to use it for a few days while he was out of town. (Otherwise they each sprang for cheap hotels, being newly arrived in the city. Apparently there was a crepuscular world of drifting girls who would sign on with an escort agency wherever they landed.) I must have come back with her from a rock and roll club. I wasn't a customer, anyway. At the man's house we'd drunk a bottle of his Chambord liqueur and Liva was concerned about replacing it. She inhabited a mental space where it actually applied that to live outside the law, you must be honest. Though I didn't realize she was a prostitute for a little while. We were peers anyway, and soon girlfriend-boyfriend. Before long I invited her to stay with me, and anything she had was mine too.

Life with Liva was to "wander like children in a Paradise of sadness." Her sad frequent difficulties (which didn't happen to include drug dependency) were always passing inconveniences to her, though, while my addiction felt like a downfall even as I embraced it. Mine was a kind of surrender to life that was an acknowledgment of defeat even if I believed it was inevitable and written into my being, and that the defeat was more true to existence than illusory "success." Part of the experience was a rejection of belief in the value or meaning of any activity, except to commune with junk.

I hawked in music clubs my distracted imitation of my original self, and I took cheap acting jobs, and pocket money for my newspaper column, and did various other small-time culture hustles (while also summoning everything I could in the writing and recording of new songs when possible), and she took phone calls that assigned her meetings with men.

She had a whole child-style personal mythology of her relationship with the world. It was almost as if she was a tribesperson from precivi-

With Johnny Thunders and Sid Vicious, New York City, late.

lization who'd found herself in the twentieth century and managed to evolve ways of navigating it. She couldn't do any work that required dealing with unexpected contingencies because she had no powers of accepted logic, and she wasn't capable of menial, unskilled labor because it was too boring and people were mean about her incompetence even there. That left her with her sexual resources, a simple knowledge on which she could rely for survival and some independence. The world was stormy but she had an umbrella. She referred to herself as Liva Paply, the "Paply" referring to *"parapluie,"* "umbrella" in French. She had a word for hard times and zones of danger and meanness too: "malaca." There is a cluster of small Indonesian islands called the Moluccas, just west of New Guinea. I think maybe she had some bad experiences there. Also, the word just sounds like bad luck.

Everything that happened to her was weather. She couldn't understand it and couldn't control it, and so didn't get deeply upset about it. That was part of what was moving about her, that childlike condition that could also be seen as a normal healthy way of surviving in a relentlessly poor environment. Her personality broke my heart and filled me with happiness. Mostly happiness. On one hand it sometimes seemed so sad that a person as full of life and devoid of malice as she was would suffer the things she did. She once came back with a bruised face from a job she took, and which got me money for drugs. When she got home she cried, which hardly ever happened. She'd been sent to find a trailer-truck driver in the cab of his vehicle parked in SoHo, where she'd had to give him a blow job, and he'd hit her in the face. We lay in bed together in the morning daylight and it was like breathing sadness, like being cut open. On the other hand, we had some money now and I could get drugs for another day.

By early 1983, I was at my wit's end regarding drugs. There had been so many cycles of suffering through withdrawal and then instantly succumbing again that it was impossible to kid myself anymore. The final turning point happened one night when I was staying with Cookie. I knew where she kept the stash of drugs she sold and I took it. It was her means of livelihood. She was a friend and I'd stolen from her. That was unacceptable, and it didn't help that she seemed less upset about it than I was. I couldn't stand being that person, a cliché owned by narcotics, who by that token couldn't be trusted even by his closest friends. I had to stop fooling myself and focus on overcoming my habit above all.

As it happened, Lizzy was in town that spring. She offered to help by nursing me in any way necessary at the apartment she'd gotten in Yorkville, on the Upper East Side. I stayed there with her and she was an angel of mercy. I went for some weeks without narcotics, though there was plenty of drinking and dope smoking. I was as mentally confused as I was physically, but Lizzy was patient compassion, always letting me know she expected nothing but only wanted to help however she could.

As ever, when we were together we understood that our relationship was primal and indestructible; that knowledge underlay all other facts of our lives. It wasn't even dramatic, it was just a law of the natural world. We had a rapport and a bond that was profound without any conditions, or even a lot of consequences. It was like we were a culture of two—it didn't require any initiative for us to make a harbor for one another, which required no maintenance or acknowledgment to sustain it and carried no responsibilities.

But, lying in bed one evening, we decided to get married. It was just a curious other way of considering what we were to each other. We'd talked about getting married a few times over the years and once had decided to do it but then I'd lost nerve. Now it seemed like conditions were different enough from anything they'd ever been before that it sounded interesting again. I suppose that marriage represented a sign of renewal to us, and an idea of maturity, or even a funny backdoor perversity, and public proclamation, we liked. There was some way it satisfyingly knitted together the threads of the previous ten years.

Lizzy was due to make an album with local black musicians in South Africa. She'd be down there for a couple of months. She had to return to Paris to finish up arrangements and then she and Michel would be off to Soweto. Michel offered me the use of his Paris apartment while they were gone.

My booking agent/manager, Singerman, was really a solid guy. He had old-fashioned ideas of loyalty and he also believed in my talent. He was not the classic intimidator type of music-business manager. He worked hard and he thought up angles, but he didn't have the aggressive ruthlessness it takes to make it in that business. He was more like Woody Allen in *Broadway Danny Rose*, trying to get bookings for the lady with the costumed parrots. He handled a lot of the striving new underground groups, like the Fleshtones and Gun Club and the Bush Tetras. It was OK for me because I was more or less his top act. I confided to him my plans with Lizzy. I told him I wanted to take advantage of Michel's offer and spend a few months in Paris, away from drugs, sealing my freedom from them and focusing on the writing of the book I had in mind (a version of Jake's road-trip book). When Lizzy returned from Africa, we'd get married. Singerman agreed to bankroll the trip. He'd advance me all expenses for Paris.

Michel had a gorgeous, classically Parisian two-bedroom apartment on the rue de Rivoli. It was all high ceilings and vintage woodwork,

Later.

painted white, with an art nouveau fireplace, a black leather Corbusier chaise longue, an excellent sound system, and classic French windows that opened onto shallow balconies railed in ornate cast iron. Doubtless it subconsciously reminded me of the late-Picasso Riviera mansion that beckoned from *Life* magazine when I was a little boy entranced by that image of the artist's life. On the apartment building's ground floor were a bar-café and a pâtisserie. It was a short walk to the Île Saint-Louis, the Bastille, Les Halles, and the Marais.

I arrived, and within two days Michel and Lizzy departed for South Africa, leaving me there alone. I didn't really know anyone else in Paris except for Michel's broody and nervous twenty-two-year-old girlfriend, Catherine, whom I'd just met.

Within another three days it was clear my plan was a disaster. I was suffering without drugs, drinking wine all day, at a loss as to what or how to write—even though I'd been commissioned by *Libération* to do a column—and desperately lonely. I didn't know how to live without drugs. They were all I could think of. I went out on dates with Catherine. I lay with her in bed. She couldn't speak English but she idolized me. She was the victim of a myth of the romantic artist, which, along with some kind of fantasy that she must have constructed from Michel and Lizzy's references to me, led her to believe that I was a god of poetry and soul-substance. We spent nights together engaged in heartbroken, desperate clutching, up to the border of actually taking full responsibility for the practice, of going all the way. It was excruciating. She had the noble melancholia of French feminine inwardness and yearning, and the appearance for it, with a long narrow nose, plump creased lips, and skeletal huge dark eyes, altogether Isabelle Adjani. There was virtually no verbal communication between us, but she adored me because I was the isolated tragic poet. We were alone, washed up on the shore of the apartment together. It drove me crazy. Her large breasts swelling against my chest. Her tears and adoration.

I was supposed to be writing a book in beautiful Paris, on my manager's ticket, awaiting the return of my future wife, who'd gotten me the lovely apartment.

I thought of another girl I could call!

In the early spring of that year I'd taken a Voidoids version to England and our British agency had assigned us a keeper named Ava, who was only sixteen. Ava was a riot, a foul-mouthed, speed-loving, pompadoured adventuress who shared a flat with another poverty-stricken speed-freak girl, a blonde in her early twenties who had a fetish for pubescent boys. She didn't like any man over thirteen. But that's another story. Ava and I had had spectacular romps in London and it occurred to me that she'd probably love to deliver some meth to me and enjoy a little Paris interlude. I wasn't wrong. She caught the next boat train.

I bent her all over the Corbusier. We were in our element. There's a point where extreme, knowing drug abandon becomes a kind of delicious hell. You are in agony psychologically, and the drugs are like an act of infinite troubling detail, as if you're making a perfect living mosaic of yourself in another state than the agony that is the reality. It's like a ballet performed at 1/1000 speed and that's how I put my granite hard-on into Ava and watched her face and watched her lips as she said something snotty and grateful to me, grinning, and meanwhile Lizzy was in the back of my mind and my heart was breaking, drily and brittle though, not as if I had any meaning to lose. It is quite possible for nothing to have any meaning.

Finally Michel and Lizzy came back. I don't know how or exactly what got revealed, but my failure and betrayal were not hidden whatsoever. It was the first and only time in all the years I knew Lizzy when everything was ice-cold and shut down. I can't even say whether she might well have had her own affairs in Africa. Though we intended to get married I'd not asked any oaths of her. But there was no question that I had betrayed us, I had betrayed myself, and I had undercut everything, it was mean and awful, and beyond discussion. I had shown myself to be a fluttering wisp of no use except as a source of pain and pathetic irritation. It had all been an illusion, because I had no substance. That's how it seemed to me. Lizzy didn't say much.

I returned to New York.

This is the end of the story of my life up until I stopped playing music and stopped using drugs. A few months after I returned to New York from Paris, I finally, against all the resistance of my pride, attended a Narcotics Anonymous meeting. Beautiful Victoria, a sometime girlfriend I'd known since the early CBGB days, had cleaned up in NA and she persisted in urging me to try it. I fled the first meeting I attended, horrified that a stranger had approached me part of the way through and hugged me. On Victoria's reassurances, and for lack of any better ideas, I eventually tried again. On the second or third meeting, it took. I came to see the practicality of NA and I stayed with it, and I left music at the same time, knowing how pervasive and tempting drugs were in that line of work. There was a two-or-three-year period of relapse at the end of the eighties and in the earliest nineties, but apart from that, I've had no drug problem since.

Once I'd cleaned up and left music, I had to figure out a new way to make a living. I experimented a little but decided within a few years that the only satisfying possibility was to become a professional writer, which is what I did.

I have chosen this cutoff point for the book because it feels natural and because the closer I get in the story to the present day the more problematic it gets to describe situations frankly. Anyway, a writer's life is fairly uneventful, and, as this book concludes, every moment of a life contains all its other moments. The tale is consistent, even repetitive, enough. It doesn't need another twenty-five years.

God likes change and a joke, to paraphrase Karen Blixen, and the joke tends to be that the changes happen in a pattern returning you to everywhere you've been.

EPILOGUE

T he other night I was walking home from a restaurant when I saw Tom Verlaine going through the dollar bins outside a used-book store. I'd been surprised to see him there a few times in recent weeks. Usually I only spot him somewhere once every two or three years. In public he always holds himself nervously apart from everyone, meeting no eyes, as if he assumes everyone wants to accost him. His head and neck perch like a raggedy spooked hawk on the high bulky prospect of his middle-aged body, above the crowds, his eyes self-consciously focused on something in the distance. When I see him on the street I don't try to get his attention, but this time I was too curious to let the moment pass. What was he doing? The books in the dollar bins are as useless as they come—outdated textbooks, forgotten mass-market trash, operating manuals. I walked up to him and asked, "Finding out anything about flying saucers?" The last time I'd spoken to him in person, as opposed to a few e-mails, had been seven or eight years before. "Yes, this is the Greek edition." He grinned at me, holding out a Greek-language three-volume set of some sort, proffering it theatrically, as if it were a great, but fragile, and possibly dangerous, prize and he was an animated cartoon, like Gumby, the way he does. He smiled something else, wide-eyed, going along with the flying saucer stuff. I replied, "I hear Plato came from Pluto."* He continued to smile widely. His teeth looked brown and broken in the night light, even worse than mine (he still smokes), and his face was porous and expanded and his hair coarse gray. I turned away and walked on, shocked. We were like two monsters confiding, but that wasn't what shocked me. It was that my feeling was love. I felt grateful for him and believed in him, and inside myself I affirmed the way he is impossible and the way it's impossible to like him. It had never been any different. I felt as close to him as I ever did. What else do I have to believe in but people like him? I'm like him for God's sake. I am him.

When Tom spoke to me there outside the bookstore, it was forty-two years ago, 1969, and he was nineteen years old; we both were. His misshapen, larded, worn flesh somehow just emphasized the purity of the spirit inside. He made a bunch of beautiful recordings too. Who gives a fuck about the worldly achievers, the succeeders at conventional ambitions?

If I had died in 1984, at the point this book ends, as could easily have happened, there would have been left such scant evidence of me that my life would be mostly just a sad cautionary tale. It's by writing a book like this one that I am redeemed at all. My life is not different for having written this book—my life only comes into being by having been written here. What I have been given and what I have been and what I have and what I and what—all are only to the extent

---

* I didn't really say that. I said, "I understand Socrates came from outer space."

they all are only to the extent all are only to the all are only to all are only all are all.

We know that we are constructed of time, not of sequence, and it is impossible to write time "not of sequence," except maybe in poetic flashes. I didn't want to write about a person through time, but about time through a person.

ACKNOWLEDGMENTS

Thanks to: Libby Edelson, my glorious editor, and Kirby Kim, my magnificent agent, whose instincts and skills and commitment made this book possible; Leah Carlson-Stanisic and Steve Attardo, designers par excellence, for, respectively, the book's interior and jacket; Jonathan Lethem and Eric Simonoff, for their original acts of goodwill; Carolyn Rhodes and Babette Meyers, whose love and loyalty and generosity have meant more than they know; all the kind photographers; and the gallant Marvin Taylor and Lisa Darms and their helpful colleagues at the NYU Fales Library and its Downtown Collection.

CREDITS

TEXT